'All the stuff
Hilariously funny
Lady to hand.'

'Sanity's a rare thing for any parent, but after years of broken sleep, cold cups of tea and your meals consisting of nicking the uneaten food from your child's plate or whatever biscuits you can hide in the highest cupboard you have… you deserve the treat of a fellow parent telling it exactly like it is!'

'Hilarious truths about parenting every parent will relate to, even if they won't admit it.'

'Takes the real moments and makes them hilarious.'

Britmums.com

'Almost enough to make me want another baby. JUST KIDDING! Reading this has brought back a lot of memories, including some I thought I had successfully repressed, so thanks for that Siobhan.'

Whinge Whinge Wine

'Relatable and reassuring parenting stories. "Wetting yourself" laughter levels throughout!'

The Dempsey Diaries

THIS MUM MALARKEY

Parenting Tales from the Woefully Unprepared and
Perpetually Overwhelmed

SIOBHAN BUTEL

BARKER
BOOKS

For Orla and Ned

ONE

What have I signed up for, and when does it get easier?

Just imagine if motherhood came with a job description:

New role – Mother

Job Title: Mum-Mum-Mum-Mummy-Mummmm-MUMMMMM!!!!!!

Work Location: Based from home, but extensive travel to soft-play hell holes, Pets at Home and draughty village halls will be required.

Salary: This is an unpaid role but will involve a small contribution of approximately £202,660 per child, to be paid over the initial 18-year period. Further investment will almost certainly be required…

Hours: Permanent, full-time, on-call 24/7. Toilet breaks, food breaks, shower breaks, sleep breaks, 'I just want FIVE BLOODY MINUTES to myself!!!' breaks available at discretion of offspring.

Reports to: Whoever screams the loudest.

Essential Duties and Responsibilities: will include, but by no means be limited to: feeding, changing, burping, rocking, hugging, pureeing, cleaning, tidying, EXTENSIVE washing, surviving Rhymetime, cursing Annabel Karmel, retrieving floaters from the bathtub, Googling 'why won't my baby sleep???', ninja-vaulting over loose Lego, buying a shedload of Calpol, singing 'Old MacDonald Had a Farm', poonami management, diving for toddlers in ball pits, and trying to hold your shit together without bursting into tears when the checkout lady asks you how you are.

Education and/or Work Experience Requirements:

- No previous experience expected, but your performance will be appraised daily by complete strangers, family members, Facebook, toddler group cliques, tutting octogenarians and Piers Morgan.

- Excellent verbal communication skills: will need to be a top-drawer negotiator, adept at coming up with creative swear word alternatives on the fly and MUST possess the ability to answer: "but WHY Mummy??" 24,327 times an hour.

- Must be able to work well under pressure (ideally after two consecutive years without sleep, covered in vomit, with the smoke alarm going off and a half-naked toddler scaling the banister screaming for ice cream).

- Expert knowledge of the complete works of Justin Fletcher, Paw Patrol and Peppa Pig. Ability to instantly recall and locate any episode from such detailed descriptions as "I want the one where Peppa eats spaghetti", desirable.

Training: Feck all. From day one, you will be thrown in at the deep end with life-or-death level responsibility, with no manual. Unlimited advice from numerous sources will be offered as part of the package but will more often than not be contradictory / ominous / useless.

We look forward to welcoming you on board!

FUNNILY ENOUGH, most of those 'What to Expect When Your Hoo-Ha's Been Hijacked' and 'Mummy's First Glorious Year' parenting books seem to be missing all-important chapters to prepare you for the glaring reality of motherhood. Where, for example, is chapter 3, '*We don't put sausages behind the sofa cushions*' – *ridiculous sentences you'll find yourself saying on a daily basis.* Or how about chapter 10, '*Feral plank of anger in Aisle 3 – surviving the supermarket shop with a tantrumming toddler*'?

Which is not to say of course, that there aren't some major perks when we take on this role of a lifetime:

Additional Information: In addition to the above responsibilities, excellent hugs, belly laughs, happy tears, ferocious pride and a legitimate excuse to snuggle up on the sofa watching Disney movies all afternoon will regularly be provided. Somehow, this seems to keep us in business… ;)

Still, I think it is so, so important that every parent has a safe space, a non-judgemental community, where they can freely share both the good and the not-so-good aspects of this whole growing-and-maintaining-a-brand-new-human thing.

There was an interview doing the rounds recently with one of those *Made In Chelsea / The Only Way Is Essex /* Man-of-a-thousand-reality-TV-specials type gentleman, who had recently become a father and felt that we were all being a bit whingy about the whole affair:

"*I think parents should stop frightening people by saying that children are an absolute nightmare because that may be the case, but it's a lovely thing to do. Even if it was hard, I'd say it was easy – I like positive vibes.*"

Right-oh…

I am VERY honest about finding parenting incredibly hard work a lot of the time. I have regaled many a friend / family member / horrified eavesdropper on the number 7 bus with tales of the chicken madras shower I treated my husband to during labour, the time when I was SO tired after yet another sleep-deprived night that I managed to set fire to the bottle warmer FOR THE SECOND TIME, the importance of investing in an extra sieve for bath-time floaters 💩, and the inordinate amount of time I seem to spend wedged inside sweat-slicked tube slides and hauling myself up rope ladders in overpriced warehouses with names like Berserk and Kiddy Kingdom. I can, however, confirm that despite this, an inexplicably large number of those people have still gone on to have their very own little sleep thieves.

Maybe it's because I am equally likely to spend a good half an hour boring them to tears with a detailed account of the thousand-odd hilarious / adorable / genius antics my daughter managed to fit in before breakfast, or force them to scroll through my extensive back catalogue of photos of Orla doing something incredibly mundane, but I still thought it was worth taking 500 snaps because she was doing that really cute nose-scrunching thing. I've told everyone and their aunt about the sheer magic that was her first proper visit to Santa's Grotto at Christmas (except for the bit where she asked for a real dog… regrettably, the elves have very strict rules about livestock on the sleigh). And quite frankly, I'm delighted that spending a rainy afternoon stuffing myself with 'fun-sized' chocolate and watching *Toy Story* is once again an acceptable adulting activity.

I wouldn't insult anyone's intelligence by telling them that parenthood is easy; it's not. It's stressful, amazing, knackering, exhilarating, monotonous, surprising, messy, beautiful, frustrating, and sooo bloody emotional, all at once. And in fact, when it comes to mental health, I think it's vital that we don't sugar-coat it. Personally, I was incredibly thankful during those first few months after Orla was born (jacked up on a heady cocktail of Co-codamol and Cadburys and still adjusting to the shock of it all) to read those 'real' stories from parent bloggers and swap experiences with other mums, because I realised that it wasn't just me feeling out of my depth, overwhelmed, and massively freaked out by *In The Night Garden* (more on this psychedelic horror-show of a programme later!)

I love the bones of my child. I cannot imagine my life without her. I would, knowing everything I know, and having been shat on / sneezed on / vommed on and smacked in the face with a Paw Patrol vehicle many more times than I care to remember, do it all again.

But I'm sorry, oh-so-shiny man off the telly – one day, when you too find yourself making a hasty exit from the extortionately priced family-friendly farm over an hour's drive away because your beloved toddler PUNCHED A CHICKEN (I kid you not), there will not be enough 'positive vibes' in the world to prevent you from quietly muttering an obscenity or two about this parenting journey we've all embarked on.

So anyway, inspired by the greats (*Hurrah for Gin, The Unmumsy Mum, Man vs Baby*, all of whom I would urge you to check out), I started my own parenting blog a few years ago, which has now become this book. Whether you're new to this or here to reminisce about the rip-roaring preschool years, I hope it gives you a giggle, sounds somewhat familiar, and reminds you that you're not going through this mum malarkey alone.

TWO

My birth story (sorry, Linda)

So, my husband Jordan and I had bought all the gear, filled the freezer with batch-cooked goodness and finally finished packing the hospital bag. I'd completed my birth plan (**ALL THE DRUGS PLEASE!!** underlined several times), and dutifully attended the antenatal classes.

Just to digress a bit here, did anybody else find those classes a bit bizarre?

Don't get me wrong, they were definitely worth going to; we picked up lots of tips, made a couple of great friends, and there were unlimited Hobnobs, which is the best way to get any kind of party started (quick note for any international readers; a Hobnob is an awesome biscuit, not some kind of embarrassing medical condition).

Superior snacks aside, it was an interesting mix of useful information and truly cringeworthy team-building games. Some highlights for you:

- At the beginning, we had to go around the circle, introduce ourselves and share the most interesting fact we could think of about our significant other. One guy, having had a good five minutes to think about it, opted for *this is Claire – she's just finished a really big cross-stitch of an owl.* Fuck me, it must be wall-to-wall fun at Claire's!

- We were then split up into two groups. The mums had to brainstorm what they found most difficult about being pregnant. FYI, screaming *"I MISS WINE!!"* straight off the bat here probably isn't the best way to go, particularly in a group whose top peeve was not being able to spend as much time at the gym. #OutOfMyDepth

- Meanwhile, the dads had been given some 'empathy bellies' to help them understand how back-breakingly uncomfortable growing a person is. We returned to the room to find three heavily pregnant men engaged in a full-on press-up competition – yup, just oozing empathy there, lads…

- On to the question-and-answer session, which Claire's other half won hands-down with: *Do the hospitals provide those squeezy bottles that you rinse your vagina with when you go to the toilet after labour, or should we pack one?* Now, I can't knock his research skills (I certainly could have done with one of these bottles) but I WISH I could have captured the look on my husband's face when confronted with that level of detail. You have to bear in mind that the only question *he'd* asked so far was how much the car park was likely to cost…

- The midwife hosting our sessions proved to be the master of understatement; she described labour as a process that would 'smart a bit' and make us feel 'rather tetchy' towards the end (no shit, Sherlock). Her grand finale was an enlightening birth demonstration featuring a dolly and a wooden pelvis, which she ended abruptly with; *I won't push the doll all the way through today, because it's a bugger to get out again*. Thanks love, I think my womb just winced.

- Ahhh, the 'real life' activities. Newsflash: spooning a blob of baby food into a doll's nappy and asking us to change it IS NOT adequate parenting preparation. I propose a slightly more realistic exercise – smear the gunk ALL the way up Sally Doll's front and back, attach her to some kind of revolving table, then get changing. In the dark. With the wipes just out of reach. Whilst someone screams in your ear and a toy that you absolutely loathe plays 'Twinkle Twinkle' at 120 decibels. *Now* we're getting somewhere!

- At the end of the class, they dimmed all the lights, played the *Twilight* theme tune and asked our partners to hold our bellies whilst staring lovingly into our eyes and contemplating the magic unfolding within. I took one look at the horrified expression of the guy behind us and spent the entire time snorting with laughter into

Jordan's shoulder – hopefully it just looked like
we were *really* into it…

Anyway, where was I? Ah yes – the to-do list was
ticked, I had nested with the best of them, we were
officially 'READY'.

'Twas the night before my due date and I was so
impatient for everything to just START. As far as I could
tell, there was naff all happening; no 'show', no 'drop', no
twinges, nowt. So, I made one last attempt to speed things
along with a lip-burning chicken madras from the local
Indian and resigned myself to another week or so of
waddling about covered in coconut oil and feeling sorry for
myself.

Fast-forward to my regular 2am toilet trip, and it
turned out that my midwife had massively downplayed the
whole 'slow trickle of fluid' waters-breaking experience… I
could easily have hosed down a burning building with my
lady bits if the need had arisen! I shouted for Jordan, who
took one look at the carnage unfolding in the bathroom
and felt that now was a sensible time to point out what a
waste of money the mattress protector we'd bought had
turned out to be…

THIS WAS IT! I couldn't believe it was finally
happening; we were actually going to meet our little girl.
Now for the long wait whilst the contractions slowly built
and we moved closer and closer towards the pointy end of
labour.

Or not.

From the get-go, my contractions were coming every
four or five minutes, and they absolutely floored me. I
couldn't believe it; I'd done my *One Born Every Minute*
research – where were those precious hours of idly flicking
through magazines gasping at the latest celebrity nose job

and bantering with my loved ones? I felt cheated. And nauseous… which was the point at which we were reunited with the chicken madras, and my husband was suitably punished for that mattress-protector comment.

We called the hospital and the lady at the desk (let's call her Laidback Linda), advised that it was absolutely normal and there was no point at all in coming in until at least 9am, as I wouldn't be anywhere near ready for the next stage yet.

At this point, I was convinced that I was the biggest wimp in the universe for finding it so tough going already, but battled on for another hour before demanding that Jordan check back in with the lovely Linda:

"*Have you tried paracetamol?*"
Jordan – "It doesn't really seem to be doing the trick, Linda…"
Me – "Yes, Linda, it's on the fecking floor, in a pool of regurgitated madras, so unless the spicy spew fumes currently engulfing the bathroom have magical medicinal properties, it's unlikely to hit the spot…"

"*How about a warm bath?*"
Jordan – "She says it's not really helping, Linda…"
Me – "Ahhhhh tepid water… are you actually shitting me, Linda? What do you do if someone breaks their leg; stick it in a sodding bucket and watch their troubles just melt away?"

"*Could she try a different position?*"
Jordan – "Actually, she does seem a bit happier in this one, Linda…"
Me – (middle finger aloft) "FUCK YOOUUUUUUUU LINDA!!!"

Just to be clear, I wasn't actually allowed to talk to Linda (a wise move on Jordan's part), and I'm reasonably confident that she couldn't hear me. Also, Linda was obviously a perfectly nice woman just trying to do her job, but in my head, she was the gatekeeper denying me entry to the place where all the drugs are kept, so basically Satan...

Anyhoo, we (I) elected to completely ignore Linda and set off to the hospital at around 5am, a 20-minute joyride of alternate vomiting and mooing (I have no idea who told me that mooing helped, but it genuinely did).

When we arrived, they gave my nether regions the once-over to see how things were progressing; it turned out that I was already 8 centimetres dilated (*Get Linda in here RIGHT NOW, I want her to SEE this*) – I immediately felt much less wimp-like.

And then, at long last, it was time for the gas and air.

Oh. My. God.

That stuff is bloody amazing. Suddenly, the contractions were bearable; I was coping, I was able to hold conversations again, I was actually doing it – *One Born Every Minute* stylee! I even called a few friends to update them on my progress; I can only imagine what they made of being woken up at stupid o'clock by someone COMPLETELY off their tits on laughing gas who kept cutting them off mid-sentence to moo...

Before I knew it I was fully dilated and ready to push – I was elated, we'd be home by lunchtime at this rate!

Or not.

She'd turned. I pushed and pushed for hours to no avail – I hit the wall, and I felt like a complete failure: was this my fault for not sitting in the right positions for the last month; had the baby heard me berating Linda and decided to crawl back to safety?

But, somehow, I kept finding one extra push. Finally, with a bit of help from a ventouse, Orla arrived at 1:32pm; eight pounds three ounces of squishy gorgeousness. She was perfect. My husband, who hadn't shed a tear the entire time I'd known him (I almost stomped back down the wedding aisle when he failed to break down appropriately at the sight of me), was in floods. We had 'the moment'.

This was immediately followed of course by the realisation that I was absolutely shattered, overwhelmed, and a bit of a fecking state to be honest (delightfully, all the blood vessels in my face had burst with the effort of pushing, which explained the slight recoil of horror when visitors first came a-calling – another fun omission from the baby books).

Ordinary things like a hot shower and buttery toast were suddenly elevated to sheer bliss.

I felt a wave of panic when Jordan had to leave the ward for the night – an actual person had spent the best part of a day cannon-balling their way out of my uterus, and now I was on night duty as well? Thankfully, the nurses were fantastic, stepping in when my fumbling fingers failed me on my first nappy change and whisking her off for a couple of hours so I could finally get some sleep.

And when I woke up, there she was, and we were alone together for the very first time. I think that was when it hit me that I'd actually done it. I was someone's mother.

Bloody hell.

So, did I take anything away from this experience, besides Orla of course and the fact that Linda probably deserves a medal if that's the kind of crap she has to deal with every day?

Well, it certainly wasn't the birth I planned or hoped for, but I think a lot of people feel like that. I know that one of my friends who had a caesarean felt somehow 'lesser' because she hadn't gone through the whole contractions / pushing experience, which is obviously nonsense. But luckily the outcome WAS everything I'd hoped for, and it's strangely true that whilst I haven't forgotten what flipping hard work it all was, I can no longer remember how those contractions really felt, even though at the time I thought they would be permanently etched into my soul.

And, I can honestly say that the thought of giving birth again wouldn't put me off having a second one. However, I can't promise the same applies to the sleepless nights and poonami nappies that swiftly followed...

THREE

So I made a tiny human... now what?

Which brings us to the early baby days. Wow, they were something.

I remember watching Harry and Meghan's TV interview after they presented their firstborn to the queen. And of course, the reporter's first questions were those immortal lines:

Is he sleeping well?

Is he a good baby?

With a few years of parenting under my belt at that point, I rolled my eyes so hard I nearly gave myself concussion...

He's TWO AND A HALF DAYS OLD, man! How the feck would they know?? I've literally spent more time staring longingly at the unclaimed chocolate eclair in the fridge at work than they've been able to spend with him yet.

And good at WHAT, exactly?? What key skills would you expect someone a third-of-a-week old to have added to their CV by now? Kayaking? Defence Against the Dark Arts?

FYI – he's probably sleeping like a newborn baby. So, a lot. Give it a few weeks and he'll be waking a lot more, and sleeping a lot less, and before they know it, they'll be watching back-to-back episodes of *Twirlywoos* at 2am, blearily inhaling family bags of Quavers and Googling 'how to stop a toddler twatting about all night' whilst he prances around the living room in his royal underwear singing, *"IIIIIITTTTTT'S MORNING TIME!!!"*

I have to be completely honest – the first few months (ok, if I'm being REALLLLYYY honest, make that the first year) of being a mum absolutely floored me mentally, physically and emotionally. In everyday life I have a busy job with a lot of responsibility. I always have about 20 different projects on the go, am a bit of a perfectionist, BIG fan of lists and planners... you know, the kind of person who's a lot of fun at parties if they know the schedule beforehand. That all went completely to pot when I became a mother. I was completely and utterly conquered by the chaos and uncertainty and sheer *relentlessness* of it all.

It turned out that there were many startling omissions in those parenting guides and websites that I had earnestly combed through in the weeks leading up to my due date. These gems, for starters:

- I spent far too much time worrying about my boobs and stretch marks, and totally neglected to consider the postpartum consequences of squeezing something the size of a watermelon down my birth canal; ice packs, rubber rings, tea tree oil... be prepared, ladies!

- From now on, whenever you're in the shower, you'll be *convinced* you can hear your baby screaming, even when they're not. Unless *Psycho* happens to be your go-to chill-out movie, this really sucks, as it's often the only chance for a bit of peace and quiet you'll get all day.

- Babies spend 90% of their time finding new and interesting ways to give you a heart attack. That periodic breathing crap they pull, their ability to turn bright purple on a whim… Orla also went through a delightful phase of suddenly stopping everything she was doing, staring into an empty corner of the living room and waving in a horrifying 'I see dead people' fashion. It's totally fine, though. I didn't fancy sleeping for the rest of my life anyway…

- It's entirely possible to be absolutely maxed out, yet incredibly bored at the same time. There was a period of time (let's call it the 6-to-12-week shitstorm), when the only way that I could get Orla to stop crying was to walk her around the bathroom for HOURS on end with the tap running. Here's an interesting fact; there are exactly 322 tiles on my bathroom walls. Consider your world rocked!

- Lullabies are COMPLETELY unfit for purpose. They're all about 10 seconds long, max. Show me a mother who can get a colicky child to sleep by the last bar of 'Hey Diddle Diddle', and I'll show you a bloomin' liar. In the end, I had to resort to a chilled-out version of that perennial favourite, 'The 12 Days of

Christmas' – she was usually out for the count before the lords started a'leaping, thankfully!

- It's a great idea to batch cook and freeze lots of meals in advance. It's also worth asking yourself if you'd be happy to eat them A – with one hand, B – freezing cold, and C – in under 45 seconds (the answer, of course, is D – all of the above).

- And finally, when it comes to nappy clean-up operations, cotton wool balls are utter shite. Unless you've always longed for a child with the face of an angel and the arse of a sheep – in which case, they're flippin' fantastic...

I have this incredibly vivid memory of walking Orla around our local park in her pram when she was about a month old *(reader – it will come as absolutely no surprise that she was screaming at the time)*, and the tears were just coursing down my cheeks. I thought to myself 'I don't know if I can do this. If I can JUST get to the six-week mark, I'll be ok'. I have no idea now what the significance of six weeks was, but I just had to keep setting myself these milestones to feel like I was moving through it all, edging towards the light at the end of the tunnel, even if it was just baby steps.

The hardest part was that everyone else on the planet appeared to be born to the role. My social media feeds seemed to be crammed with perfectly groomed mummies clutching smiling tots at sunlit picnics in the park, an event that was seamlessly slotted in between baby massage and rhymetime classes; effusive odes to the joys of motherhood scattered liberally with #Blessed and #TimeOfMyLife and #WouldntChangeAThing. For me, just leaving the house and putting one foot in front of the other seemed a gargantuan effort most days. A lot of the time, I just felt like I was failing at something that was supposed to come naturally to me.

The thing is, though, once I started my blog, I realised it wasn't just me at all. I got so many messages from other mums who also found it a struggle and felt incredibly guilty about not loving every waking moment of being a parent. We really just need to TALK about it more and be more open with each other about the downs, as well as the ups.

I went to a good friend's baby shower about a year after Orla was born, and it really got me thinking. It was the first one I'd been to since having her, and pre-baby me and post-baby me definitely had very different reactions (*internal*, I feel it is important to stress here) as the gift giving commenced:

Mum-to-be unveils gorgeous tiny dress / tights / cardigan / bootie ensemble

Pre-baby me: Oooh, so adorable!

Post-baby me: Fuck that for a game of soldiers! After your fifth 'bum-to-neck' poo of the day, deliciously sandwiched between two sneak-attack wees and three out-of-the-blue vomiting sessions, you'll be hot footing it down to Tesco for as many cheap sleepsuit multipacks as you can squeeze into your trolley.

Mum-to-be struggles to maintain her level of enthusiasm as she unwraps yet another set of bibs and muslins

Pre-baby me: We really should have all coordinated

beforehand, we've massively overdone it on the dribble-catcher front.

Post-baby me: There is NO SUCH THING as too many bibs or muslins; there WILL be a point when every radiator / banister / family member in the house will be draped with the bloody things, and you'll still have to resort to using the nearest tea towel / cushion / item of your husband's clothing for emergency damage control.

Mum-to-be coos over tiny pack of scratch mitts

Pre-baby me: What a useful gift!

Post-baby me: BAHAHAHAHAHAHAHA! (big congrats if you cracked the mystery that is shoehorning tiny flailing hands into these ridiculous contraptions without them being unceremoniously thrown across the room seconds later, but I never did).

Anyhoo, the part that I really struggled with was during the grand finale of the shower, when we each had to write down a little 'pearl of wisdom' for my friend in a keepsake book.

What on earth do you say???

I didn't want to freak her out too much, so resisted the urge to walk her through my postpartum lady-bits regime… I also vowed that I would never join the 'one day you'll miss all this' / 'everything is a phase' / 'before you know it you won't even remember the early days' brigade because, whilst all irritatingly true, being told so when I was eyeballs-deep in nappies and mess and exasperated tears (mine, the baby's, take your pick), made me want to punch people in the face. Really hard.

So that left me with this.

There will probably be times over the next few days and weeks and years when you feel like you're making a bit of a hash of this whole raising a tiny human thing. I just want you to know that you're not alone.

It's completely normal to regularly feel like a complete idiot. Pre-Orla, I felt like a together, can-do kind of human. Post-Orla, I can count on one hand the number of times I've actually managed to do up a babygrow without having a fecking popper left over, despite changing her at least 15 times a day. Other highlights include spraining my ankle tripping over a Teletubby, getting Orla completely redressed and only then realising I realising I'd forgotten to put another nappy on her, and sobbing down the phone to my husband because I couldn't remember how to undo the release catch on the pram. The pram I insisted on because it was so easy to fold up and open…

You're doing an amazing job. If she's fed, warm, clean (relatively), and you can't recall how many kisses you've given her that day, take the win. In the meantime, take a deep breath, grab that bottle of wine I gave you at the baby shower (now THAT's a practical gift) and call me. xxx

And it really does get better. What's strange now is that those things that seemed all-consumingly insurmountable at the time, whether it be the trapped wind or the difficult feeds or the 'I WOULD SELL MY SOUL FOR TWO CONSECUTIVE HOURS OF SLEEP', are whispers of a distant memory. It's bizarre how little of the detail of it all I can actually remember. There simply came a time when the dishes had been washed, the sun was out, I was blowing raspberries on her tummy and looking forward to a playdate with a friend that afternoon, and it just crept up on me that I was feeling good. I was awake. I was doing this. The highs really did outweigh the lows.

The absolute best advice I can give you if you're enveloped in the newborn fug right now and finding it tough, aside from talking to someone, is to be kind to yourself. It's SUCH a steep learning curve and there is no right or wrong way of doing it, no guarantees that one mum's 'life-saver' of a tip will work for every baby, and not one person out there who hasn't sat on the kitchen floor and had a good cry about this whole parenting palaver at some point, no matter what they're hashtagging on Facebook.

Here's something I wrote on my blog a couple of years back on the importance of giving yourself a bit of a break when you fail to live up to your own parenting expectations:

I thought I'd be a mum who took it all in her stride. But I wasn't.

I was a mum pushing a pram in the driving rain, crying my eyes out and wondering how on earth I was going to get through the next few weeks, let alone years.

I hoped I'd be a mum who'd say airily "oh, she'll eat ANYTHING put in front of her!" But I'm not.

I'm a mum who has seriously considering handing my food shop straight over to the binmen just to save time, and is slightly concerned that Orla will think ALL dinosaurs were breadcrumbed and made from turkey…

I thought I'd be a mum who strode confidently back into work in pristine business attire.

But more often than not, I'm a mum with butter on my trousers, tomato sauce in my hair, and Peppa Pig stickers on my arse.

I thought I'd be a soft-play boss, not the sweaty, panting, panicking mum firmly wedged between two slightly whiffy foam rollers.

I hoped I'd be a mum who kept on top of the housework, and ALWAYS kept her cool. But I'm not.

I'm a mum who has to pop into the kitchen to let out the 'mum rage' and hasn't seen the living-room floor for about 18 months.

I hoped I'd be a mum who 'cherished every moment'. It turns out, some moments are a little bit shit.

BUT…

*I **AM** a mum who gets up again every morning and heads once more into the breach; who knows all of Orla's ticklish spots; who would get 100% in a Paw Patrol quiz; who powers on through a dead arm when commando-crawling away from the cot after FINALLY getting her to sleep; who will get that sodding muffin tin out of the cupboard ONE more time in the hope that this time, she'll actually try the homemade toddler-friendly quiches, and I am the mum she always runs to when the world gets a little bit scary.*

And I've decided that I'm OK with that. Because life's too short to beat myself up for not being the mum I thought I'd be, when there are plenty of reasons to be proud of the mum that I am.

#WeveGotThis

FOUR

It takes a village

After you've had a baby, it's virtually impossible to get from A to B without being intercepted by at least a dozen well-meaning strangers keen to have a gander at the fruit of your loins and impart some grade-A parenting wisdom.

Here are some of my favourites from the early days:

"YOU MUST CHERISH EVERY MOMENT!"

I'm fully aware of how lucky we are to have our lovely little girl, and that there will come a time when me walking through the door will no longer be the highlight of her day, and when I can't solve every heartache with a cuddle and a Kinder Egg. But I'm sorry, I just can't treasure EVERY moment. Like when she shat in the bath. Or when she had an epic tantrum because I wouldn't let her climb into the oven. Or when I'm watching Bing at 2am. I think it's OK not to treasure those moments...

"IS YOUR HUSBAND BABYSITTING TONIGHT?"

No, no he isn't. Last time I checked he's not a teenager looking for some work experience, I don't pay him to watch her, and he doesn't spend the majority of the evening texting his mates and raiding the fridge for snacks (OK, the last part's pretty accurate). He's *shock horror* looking after **HIS OWN CHILD** whilst mummy drinks Prosecco with her friends and tries REALLY hard to think of something interesting to talk about other than her daughter and all related topics (which is tricky, because all we seem to watch these days is CBeebies and I can't remember the last book I read that didn't involve lifting flaps and locating farmyard animals).

"OH, SHE'S A GIRL?!?"

Always said in a slightly accusatory manner, implying that I'd somehow failed in my motherly duty to label my offspring appropriately for the benefit of passers-by. I hate to disappoint, so I'd advise anyone with a similar dilemma to ensure that before you leave the house you give your little darling a good dunking in glitter, braid a small herd of My Little Ponys into her hair and rig the pram to play 'Girls Just Wanna Have Fun' when anyone walks past… that should cover it!

"I CAN GO AND CHECK WHAT WE HAVE IN THE GIRLS' SECTION?"

Leading on from the above, this was the time a shop assistant was rather puzzled by my choice of a dinosaur sleeping bag for Orla… Seriously, love?

One – the 'girl' ones had butterflies on them – I bloody hate butterflies. I had a panic attack at a butterfly farm once; why on earth people find being mobbed by a pack of winged beasties an enjoyable family day out, I'll never know.

Two – the dinosaur one was 50% off – this is a pretty big deal. I can only assume that grobags are woven by fairies, hand-washed by mermaids and then gently blown dry by unicorns before they reach the shelves, given the extortionate price charged for what is essentially a sack with straps.

Three – and what?!? She looks awesome in blue, she loves dinosaurs, and surely there were girl dinosaurs too? Although that *would* explain why they died out so quickly.

"IS SHE YOUR ONLY ONE?"

Now this is actually a perfectly reasonable (if slightly nosy) question, but just once, I'd like to react by looking around wildly, shouting *"Oh bugger it, I've left Tipsy-Lou in Argos again"* and tearing off in the opposite direction…

"HAVING A CHILLED ONE TODAY?"

No, Mr Chugger, standing oh so hopefully on my doorstep, I am bloody well not. The reason I am wearing my dressing gown at 3.30pm is that my daughter has been vomiting for two days straight, and the only other item of clothing I own that isn't currently coated in sick is a 'Sexy Pirate' Halloween costume, which is a tad risqué for a Wednesday afternoon. And I don't know about you, but I very rarely 'chill' by watching back-to-back episodes of *Postman Pat* at an ear-splitting volume whilst frantically wet-wiping Happyland Farm animals (who haven't got an awful lot to be happy about since getting caught in that torrential spew shower after lunch).

Suffice to say, he swiftly took his clipboard elsewhere.

People-you-don't-even-bloody-know aside, a further aspect of having a child that I really didn't anticipate was the seismic impact it has on your relationship with your partner. During pregnancy it's all eager expectation as you huddle together on the sofa to feel the baby kick, fondly imagining tranquil family walks and quiet snuggles before bedtime. But for me, one of THE hardest things about having a baby was going from 'husband and wife' to 'mum and dad'. You're both sleep deprived, completely out of your depth, and your temper is on a knife edge. It's the ultimate relationship test.

Pre-baby, we'd spend weekends visiting friends, trying new restaurants and staying up until the wee small hours debating anything and everything (usually completely irrelevant topics like how many members of Eternal there originally were. *"It's four, it's BLOODY four!!! I don't care that it's 1am, I'm Googling it…"*)

Fast forward a year or so and 50% of the texts you're sending each other are purely focused on the contents of your little darling's nappies (I've checked; they make for a thrilling read!) and most evenings are spent dashing around ticking off dinner / bath / bedtime-related jobs before collapsing on the sofa to indulge in the inevitable *who's the most tired today* parenting pissing contest. And on top of that, I'm the first to admit that I was a hormonal mess for many, many months after Orla was born – the smallest thing would set me off. I remember crying bitterly for a full half-hour because I couldn't get the lid off the Sudocrem. Crying over fecking bum cream! I must have been a joy to live with.

I've got to hand it to him, though, Jordan really stepped up to the plate too, whether that meant holding her hand all night so that we all got a decent night's kip, or doing an emergency wine run (a not uncommon occurrence).

He was also infinitely more patient with her than I was. He'd happily read *In the Night Garden: Everybody Loves Christmas* over and over again (in my defence, it was chuffing MARCH and she was still obsessed with that sodding book), long after I'd have distracted her with something shiny and consigned the little bollocks to the kitchen drawer for the day (Igglepiggle, not the baby; that kind of thing's generally frowned upon these days).

Things calmed down a lot as she got older, but we do still drive each other mad; I find his overly-relaxed attitude to the way she constantly discovers exciting new ways to injure herself infuriating *("well, she's got to learn about edges sometime"* – *"not by running head-first into them, you muppet!")* and his 50% approach to household chores is enough to drive a girl to drink; nappies left *next to* the bin rather than in them, 40 different items 'left to soak' in a blatant attempt to avoid the washing-up, a clothes horse so stacked with washing it looks like an elaborate game of laundry Buckaroo…

BUT he's pretty much the only person interested in discussing which military organisation Major Clanger's part of, and whether Mama and Papa Wottinger feel uncomfortable getting it on in the same room as their eight children. He's seen me at my very worst (the post-birth sponge-down in the shower was really not a sexy moment), but still thinks I'm beautiful, even on the days when I have scrambled egg in my hair and an entire scout troop could comfortably set up camp in the bags under my eyes (which is pretty much any day ending in 'y'). So, all in all, I'm pretty damn grateful to have him around.

But it really does take a village to raise a child, which brings me on to the incredibly intimidating practice of 'making mum friends'. I don't know about you, but I don't think I've put any active effort into making friends since primary school, and *"my name's Siobhan, I like spaghetti hoops, wanna go on the swings?"* isn't as effective a conversation opener as it used to be.

So, I'm going to get in touch with ITV2 and pitch 'Parent Island', which is a lot like *Love Island*, but the objective is to find your perfect parenting pal for coffee mornings and WhatsApp rants. Here's how I think the drama would unfold:

– The show airs at least 24 hours later than planned when everyone refuses to get their underboobs and arse cracks out in the name of on-trend swimwear. Having spent the best part of 48 hours pushing an 8-pounder out of your lady bits, you have literally zero interest in giving yourself a front-to-back wedgie for the sake of fashion.

– Amongst a sea of footballers, firefighters and 'influencers', new islander John casually drops into the conversation that he's in charge of booking the CBeebies Bedtime Story guests, and Tom Hardy *"is a really nice guy actually"*. John is now a God. Everyone wants to be with John, or be John. John has instantly become everyone's 'type' (whereas in *Love Island* 'type' seems to be code for 'hair colour' – who knew the key to finding true love was lurking in a bottle of Tresemmé?)

– There are no midnight slanging-matches, mainly because everyone's in bed by 9pm. Not to 'do bits' or reach second base, or any of that other nonsense, they're just revelling in the pure joy that is 12 solid hours of sleep during which nobody is kicking you in the face, asking if it's morningtime yet or quizzing you on your favourite Disney Princess.

– John goes from hero to zero after accidentally revealing after one too many drinks that he thinks *Hey Duggee* is overrated and *Show Me Show Me* is compelling viewing. Nobody can stand to look at him anymore and

John is relegated to the daybed to reconsider his life choices.

– Nobody gives a damn about going into the hideaway. The luxury of being able to have a poo in peace without assorted members of your family wandering in to have a chat / sing you a song / ask you where their car keys are is the ultimate in privacy goals.

– Finally, the winners walk away with 18 years' worth of Domino's vouchers, Play-Doh-resistant furniture and 'get out of bedtime free' cards. Lucky sods...

I think the idea has real legs!

THERE'S ALSO BEEN a lot of buzz in the press about Mush and other apps to help like-minded parents find each other for local playdates and such. Inspired by this, I put together a short questionnaire to help me assemble my very own parent posse:

Q1: HOW DO YOU FEEL ABOUT ALFIE, VTECH'S EVER-POPULAR LITTLE SINGING BEAR?

A – He's both educational AND adorable! What's not to love??

B – Who the fuck is Alfie?? *(You have NO idea how lucky you are if this is you. One day you too will be given this satanic furball by a well-meaning relative, and you will **WEEP**.)*

C – If I have to sit through "I'm a friendly light-up bear, 1,2,3!" *one* more bloody time, I'm going to coat him in Pedigree Chum and feed him to next door's dog... let's see him count his way out of that one!

Q2: HOW WOULD YOU DESCRIBE YOUR LIVING ROOM STYLE?

A – Do you mean the Drawing Room?

B – I'd say it's an eclectic mix of Mid-century Modern and Olde-World charm.

C – Like Toys R Us thew up on it, then the CBeebies cast hosted an all-night, drink-fuelled orgy in it.

Q3: WHAT ONE THING DO YOU THINK YOUR LOCAL SOFTPLAY IS CURRENTLY LACKING?

A – We need at least double the number of children climbing *up* the slides and stopping everyone else from coming down. It's so key to develop their 'survival of the fittest' instincts before they hit preschool.

B – More areas that are only accessible via revolving tunnels, crawl spaces and rope ladders. You're really not in the softplay zone until you have that head-to-toe sweaty sheen going on.

C – A bar! No wait, a Prosecco bar!! No wait, a FREE Prosecco bar!!! Yup, that's the one.

Q4: WHAT'S YOUR CHILD'S FAVOURITE GAME?

A – She's a real chess whizz; she pulled the Queen's Gambit on me last time, little minx!

B – She's really more into meditating?

C – Whinge Charades – essentially, she screams and gesticulates wildly whilst you frantically try to guess what she wants before one of you starts crying. *"You want the cup? You want me to drink from the cup? You want me to put the cup somewhere else?? WHAT DO YOU WANT??!!!"*

Q5: WHAT IS YOUR FRIENDLY SUPERMARKET DELIVERY DRIVER MOST LIKELY TO SAY WHEN HE HANDS OVER YOUR BAGS?

A – "Sorry, we're all out of organic quinoa. We've substituted it for the regular kind, though?"
B – "Hang on, I'll just go grab that third bag of vegetables."
C – *Sets boxes of wine down on the counter* "Having a party?" (*No no, it's just us…*)

Q6: WHAT WAS THE LAST TEXT YOU SENT YOUR SIGNIFICANT OTHER?

A – "I miss you already… no, I love *you* more!!"
B – "Can you pop into Smyths on your way home? The wall-mounted paper distributor in the crafting zone is almost out!" (I'm looking at you, Topsy and Tim's mum!)
C – "It's been a fucking car crash today; she's trashed the place, refused to eat, non-existent naps and there appears to be a Duplo sheep bobbing about in the toilet. FML. WHEN WILL YOU BE HOME?????"

If you got mostly Cs, then yay, we're a match! So, your softplay hell hole or mine??

FIVE

Food is for fun... said no one

As your baby progresses from wrinkly newborn to babbling bum shuffler to lightning-quick crawler hell-bent on the destruction of all he or she surveys, it's safe to say that life still revolves around that Holy Trinity of eating, sleeping and shitting. I'm confident that nobody is interested in reading an entire chapter on infant bowel movements (and let's be honest, we've all spent more midnight hours than we care to admit Googling *is my baby's poo supposed to be this colour??*), so let's focus on the first two.

When I was heavily pregnant with Orla, frantically reading up on everything I'd neglected to bother even thinking about during the previous 8 months (like cramming for an exam you have absolutely no hope of passing), it genuinely never occurred to me that mealtimes might be one of the big issues. I think I just presumed that I would make something, they would eat it, and we'd all move on with our lives.

What a complete eejit.

So, if you too find yourself enthusiastically cheerleading from the highchair sidelines every evening, willing your child to eat just ONE MORE SPOONFUL of something that hasn't been dipped in E numbers and fried in sugar, here are my top tips.

- It's a scientifically proven fact that the longer you spend lovingly crafting veggie-packed, child-friendly culinary delights, the sooner you'll be scraping it all into the bin whilst your little one dry-heaves dramatically in the next room, incensed to have been presented with such slop. It's also totally okay to mutter obscenities into the bin at this point.

- Try putting their food on your own plate. Much like ex-boyfriends, snacks become infinitely more appealing when somebody else wants them. Take this to the next level by giving their food to another child. Your little angel may not want your poxy carrot sticks, but they'll go batshit crazy if you let someone else gnaw on them.

- Here's a foolproof recipe for when you have a little time on your hands. Place food items on the floor, ideally beneath the rug or sofa. Coat liberally with dust / hair / unidentifiable ick and leave to rest (about a week should do it). Kids can't get enough of that stuff. Bonus points for successful foraging sessions when the Health Visitor pops over...

- Make sure everyone else in the house is on board with the whole healthy-eating malarkey. The chances of your child finishing their dinner are dramatically reduced when *someone* (naming no names here, but he's getting feck all for Father's Day), waltzes in mid-meal with a marshmallow kebab covered in rainbow sprinkles. Dinner is now in the bin, the sprinkles are now in your hair, and Daddy's now in the doghouse. Nobody wins.

- Outsource all meals to nursery. As part of their lifelong mission to make you look like a complete bullshitter in front of other people, your child will happily wolf down mixed-bean cassoulet, or lamb and apricot tagine, basically ANYTHING that those magical nursery pixies whip up for them. Unbelievable…

- It's time to bring out the big guns, aka "Here comes the choo choo train /aeroplane / monster truck!!!" If your offspring is a fan of *Postman Pat* (rest assured, we'll be spending a lot more time on the mind-boggling world of CBeebies later on), try using one of his many vehicles here instead – he's rarely on time and always takes the most convoluted route, so with any luck you'll lull your child into a false sense of security and get a few mouthfuls in whilst you still have the element of surprise.

- If all else fails, admit defeat and opt for one of the following pre-approved food groups:

– Anything shaped like a dinosaur / smiley face /
woodland creature
– Anything battered or beige
– Anything produced by Cadbury

I also advise steering well clear of social media during
mealtimes. Facebook *really* doesn't help when you're yet
again scraping baked beans off the ceiling whilst someone
in your local Mum group shares the delightful woodland
scene they've constructed out of hummus and celery sticks
for their ravenous little healthy-eating hoard.

And don't get me started on bloody Annabel Karmel. I
once attempted her 'quick and easy' chicken curry. Prep
time – three minutes. That's three minutes to cube chicken,
peel and chop an onion, crush garlic, peel and thinly slice
an apple, quarter baby sweetcorn AND weigh out half a
dozen other ingredients.

Annabel – and I say this with the greatest respect –
you're having a fecking giraffe, love. It took me three
minutes alone to wrestle the onion away from a toddler
who was adamant it was her new best friend...

And what about eating out?

In principle, I'm a big advocate of taking young
children out to eat. I think it's really important that Orla is
regularly exposed to the experience whilst she's little, and
love that she gets the opportunity to try different flavours
and dishes. (I imagine that's also a big plus for her; the food
at Chez Mama is hardly 5 star.) In practice, though, it's a
bit of a mission.

Pre- and post-baby dining adventures are VERY
different beasts:

• Those days of simply wandering into a lovely
  bistro you've happened upon are officially dead.

Now you have to pack a flippin' suitcase full of changing gear, eating equipment and tantrum-prevention tricks before you can even leave the house; it looks like you're moving in, not stopping for a quick bite.

- There is no such thing as an evening meal anymore – you're heading back out of the door with your ketchup-covered offspring long before the pensioners start rocking up for their early-bird specials.

- Our restaurant selection criteria has also changed somewhat:

Pre-baby:
"What's the food / service/ ambience like?"

Post-baby:
"What percentage of the food is nugget shaped?"
"Is it child-friendly?" (Painfully bright / aggressively colourful / cloaked in despair)
"Are there children noisier than mine inside?"

- An empty restaurant used to be a bit of a let-down. These days, it's a real happy-dance moment. I'm all for having a smaller audience / victim pool when the shit inevitably hits the fan…

- Wooden spoons now indicate two things – your table number, and the number of times your child will repeatedly smack said utensil against the table before you completely lose your cool (*"don't do that, sweetie; no… that's enough now… look at me, don't hit the… oh for fuck's sake! It's like eating with the cast of bloody* Stomp!*")*

- Certain situations, you just learn to avoid. For example, those American diner booths have been a big no-no since Orla spent an entire meal lounging over the back of one trying to pat the head of the poor sod sitting behind us.

- Hot food is a ticking time bomb. Toddlers flippin' love it when you place a tempting plate of food in front of them, then tell them they can't touch it. Cue frantic blowing, fanning and goujon-dismantling in a bid to stem the waterworks.

- I used to think that those balloons they have near restaurant counters were a lovely touch for families. Now I know I'm in for an hour of latex bitch slaps to the face, followed by ear-splitting screams when I finally snap and confiscate the damn thing. Thanks guys, thanks a chuffing bunch.

- For adults, it's all about finger food – one hand to eat, the other to prevent your little darling from impaling herself with the cutlery / eating the complimentary crayons / lobbing breadsticks at the couple on the next table.

- Laminated menus are a winner; they're much harder to chew. Plastic glasses rule; they're much harder to smash. Dungarees are essential;

they're much easier to remove when your child's arse explodes all over the highchair…

- I end up spending way more time *under* the table searching for duplo / runaway peas / my dignity, than actually eating at it.

- There's none of that romantic feeding each other dessert nonsense from your dating days – we're mainly fending off little hands attempting to force regurgitated sweet potato fries into our mouths.

- When the waiter brings us the bill, we never get offered coffee anymore; it's almost like they don't want us to linger?

ANOTHER TOP TIP for encouraging good eating habits is getting children involved in the cooking process. Given Orla's age and my limited expertise, this has led to the production of approximately 4000 batches of wonky fairy cakes over the course of my mum life whenever the urge to 'do some fun baking' overtakes me. It's unfathomable that I've put myself through it so many times, to be honest. Here's how it usually goes down:

Step 1 – Momentarily take leave of your senses and let your child pick whatever recipe they like from your 'Simple Cakes' book (having inexplicably forgotten that you are A), pants at baking and B), working with someone who's more likely to smack you across the face with their whisk than produce anything useful with it).

Step 2 – Explain to your child that whilst 'Sangria Cake' does indeed look very pretty, it's probably not appropriate for a Mums & Tots group (not that you didn't briefly consider it – some leftover Cointreau sounds pretty fecking terrific right now).

Step 3 – Fall back on good old reliable fairy cakes, because at least you have all the ingredients for those, right?

Step 4 – Buy new ingredients: turns out you've been cohabiting with that self-raising flour at the back of your cupboard longer than you have with your husband.

Step 5 – Cream together sugar, butter, eggs, and a smidgeon of toddler sneeze for that extra 'je ne sais quoi'. Nearly dislocate your elbow in the process because it turns out 'creaming' is a lot of bloody effort and this is the exact reason why you normally stick to packet mixes with radioactive icing and those revolting 'edible' paper things that stick to the roof of your mouth.

Step 6 – In the spirit of fostering independence and creativity and all that, let your toddler add the flour. Now you, your child, and everything you own is covered in flour. Well-fecking-done, you absolute chump. WHEN WILL YOU LEARN??? Spend the next 30 minutes hosing down your nearest and dearest.

Step 7 – Grit your teeth as your child fails to locate any of the 12 available cupcake cases and opts to Jackson-Pollock the crap out of your kitchen table instead. Salvage what you can and hurl it into the oven, which should be just about hot enough now given that it's had DECADES to preheat since you started this absolute farce of an activity.

Step 8 – Try not to lose your shit when your child spends the next 8—10 minutes screaming "*CAKE-CAKE-CAKE-NOWWWW!!!*" at the oven.

Step 9 – Try not to lose your shit when your child spends the following 10 minutes screaming "*CAKE-CAKE-CAKE-NOWWWW!!!*" at the cooling rack.

Step 10 – You could not be more over this by now. It's decorating time and they're up to their neck in icing and covered head-to-toe in sprinkles: your child is basically a walking, whining, Fab lolly. As far as you can see, there's sod all on the actual cakes themselves as of yet.

Step 11 – Collapse on the sofa, eat ALL the cakes, and vow never to put yourself through such madness again (until the next rainy day, of course).

I bet Nigella doesn't have to put up with this bollocks…

SIX

Sleep is for the lucky

There are many huge 'highs' that come with having a child; the euphoria of those first smiles and steps, those midnight cuddles when the whole world stops and you just marvel at the amazing little person you somehow managed to create. But bloody hell, there are some lows – those colicky, vomity calamitous days when nothing you do seems to work, you're drowning in mess and so utterly out of it you can't even make toast without setting off the smoke alarm JUST as your baby finally nods off.

Hands-down, the biggest shock to my system was the sleep deprivation. The four-month sleep regression hit us like a freight train – seemingly endless nights of rocking and whispering and back-rubbing, then EVER SO GENTLY placing her down, only to start all over again 30 minutes later. Her first birthday came and went, and the chances of her ever getting anywhere close to 'sleeping through' seemed about as likely as a lottery win...

Thank goodness there were two of us to share the load; I have no idea how I'd have coped otherwise.

But hark, I hear a far-off braying from a tutting Facebook hoard...

"*Hang on, though – doesn't your husband work?*"

Apparently (because you can't move for '*that's not how WE did it!*' tales from the parenting coalface once you've joined the club), if one of you goes to work, the person at home is on permanent night duty. They need their rest; this is what you've signed up for – end of.

Cue those all too familiar waves of mum guilt – was I being selfish and lazy? Was I shirking 'my job' and piling too much responsibility on Jordan? I've thought about it and no, we both felt that 50/50 was absolutely the fairest way to go for us.

Of course, there are many situations where this just isn't possible. It depends on how you're feeding your baby, and the kind of job your partner has. If them not being at 100% capacity at work would endanger lives, I completely understand that a good night's sleep is paramount. And many people have no choice but to go it alone.

BUT – if it *is* possible, why on earth not?

These days we're both back at work, and when she's had a bad night it's certainly no picnic juggling spreadsheets, meetings and projects the next day. But I can safely say that days at home with her were just as exhausting, if not more so – at least at work I can go to the toilet on my own and eat a sandwich with both hands...

And the whole *but you can catch up during the day when they're asleep* thing? She was more of a 'sleep for 30 minutes at a time, if you're lucky, and you maintain the optimum level of perpetual motion and bangin' lullaby tunes throughout' kind of gal, so no, not really!

Yes, my husband's job is important, but keeping a tantrum-tastic child alive and happy and healthy and stimulated, whilst desperately clinging on to your own sanity (AND finding time for all those chores that keep the cupboards stocked and the laundry from collapsing in a heap on top of you) is pretty vital too.

Whether you're in the office or in the home, you're both working bloody hard for your family, so why does only one of you get to clock off in the evenings? Isn't it better for everyone's health and happiness if we all get regular opportunities for a bit of shut-eye?

To conclude, 50/50 for the win – I'll leave it there!

Anyway, we survived somehow and finally progressed past the 'nappy, bottle, rocking, SNEAK AWAY, nappy, bottle, rocking, SNEAK AWAY!' on repeat, for infinity, stage, only to discover the joys of bedtime once they're older and therefore articulate enough to run both verbal and actual rings around you for HOURS the very moment the clock strikes bedtime.

Sound familiar? Here's a little bedtime story for all the tired mums out there!

The Bedtime Routine

Once upon a time, Mummy had strong, unwavering views on 'the bedtime routine'. She had read the baby books, she had watched half an episode of *Supernanny*, she was sold on that immovable foundation of 'bath, book, bed'... she KNEW that consistency, patience and loving reassurance would teach her little cherub to skip off to bed with a spring in her step, a song in her heart, and a deeply ingrained desire to be fast asleep between the hours of 7pm and 7am.

Then, Mummy actually HAD a child...

Mummy has long since given up on the nightly bath, given that this tends to involve at least 15 minutes of coaxing her water-resistant offspring into it, 20 minutes of ear-shattering wails of "*IT'S IN MY EYES!!!*" and a half-dozen slippery laps around the bathroom chasing a dripping-wet 3ft streaker... NO ONE has the time or sanity for that shit every day.

Mummy has *longgggggg* since capitulated and allowed 'one book' to become 'many, many books'... Mummy turns page after mind-numbing page of 'Peppa Pig Twunts About At The Farm / Fair / Zoo', interrupted by the same gazillion questions Mummy answered yesterday:

"What's that penguin's name, Mummy?"
"What's that other penguin's name, Mummy?"
"Is that penguin the other penguin's best friend, Mummy?"
"Where's the Mummy penguin, Mummy?"
"Does Peppa Pig like penguins, Mummy?"
"Can I have a penguin, Mummy?"*

having FINALLY moved on to the next page – *"What's that, Mummy??"*

... Seriously? ... **IT'S A SODDING PENGUIN!!!** Remember?? One of those flappy little feckers we just spent 20 minutes analysing on page 3? No?? No recollection whatsoever?? Brilliant...

Mummy finally reaches her literary limit and announces that the 'bed' stage of the 3 Bs has officially begun. What has actually commenced is Mummy's rapid progression towards her 10,000 daily steps target as she traipses up and down the stairs fetching 'just one more' blanket / drink / cuddly toy / random vegetable, in her little one's quest for the perfect sleep set-up.

Eventually, Mummy tucks her little angel up tightly, plants a gentle kiss on her brow, and relishes the soft touch of that pudgy little hand on her cheek as she reaches up and whispers those three magical words...

"Need a POO!!"

Of course you bloody do...

Twenty minutes later, Mummy resumes her standard post-goodnight position, lying on the floor next to her daughter's bed trying to ignore the siren-esque lull of the white-noise machine, her only source of light the faint glow of her phone as she furiously messages her husband demanding he stop by the off-licence on the way home from work for essential supplies.

But wait – it's gone quiet. Could it be??? Mummy might even catch the end of *Bake Off*!

Mummy EVER-so-gently eases herself off the floor and slowly raises her head above the parapet... only to find herself eyeball-to-eyeball with a distinctly unimpressed *Dafuq you think YOU'RE going???* glare.

Fuuuuuuuuuck...

Mummy silently sinks back to the ground and wheels out that age-old parenting technique – 'pretending to be asleep'. Two hours and one very dead leg later, Mummy awakes with a start, victim of her own excellent acting skills. In a bleary haze, she commando-crawls with SAS-stealth across the room, rolls through the doorway, and staggers towards the light.

Success!

Drinking in the following 7.5 golden minutes of peace and Pinot Grigio, Mummy stumbles up to her own bed, pausing briefly to poke her head around the door and marvel at her beautiful daughter as she sleeps. Mummy cannot believe that she created such perfection. In fact, she can't really remember what she was so frustrated about earlier, it's all worth it in the end isn't it when you look at their little fa—

Oh crap, did she just move??? RETREAT!!!!!!

THE END (until tomorrow, suckers!)

I CAN CONFIRM, though, as someone blessed with a child who was comfortably the most unsleepy-sleeper in the history of ever (well, amongst my own family and friendship group anyway), that it *does* get better. And that you're not doing anything wrong if you are similarly blessed. We tried absolutely everything to improve her sleep: white noise, blackout blinds, earlier bedtimes, later bedtimes, changing nap times around, dropping naps, 'sleepy' foods before bed, lavender sprays for her bedding, co-sleeping, mindfulness apps, hypnotic bedtime stories, sleep experts… the works (hell, I'd have tried limboing naked in the moonlight singing 'Uptown Girl' if someone on Mumsnet had said it made *their* toddler sleep better). Some of it helped, and some of it didn't; some of it seemed to work for a while but then went out the window the second the next sleep regression hit or she cracked on to what we were trying to do (children are sneaky bedtime geniuses like that).

You could have 10 other mums trying exactly the same thing with children exactly the same age, under exactly the same scientifically controlled conditions, and you would more than likely get 10 completely different levels of success. Some children are excellent sleepers, and some are not – and that, my friend, is mostly down to the luck of the draw.

I can only assure you that there is a light at the end of the tunnel. These days, once she's exhausted her supply of critically important pre-bedtime questions such as:

"What are the prickles on my brush called?"
"Why do we only have one head?"
"Why do birds have wings but I don't have wings?"
"Why do chicken pops give you spots?"
"Where are Mr Tumble's Mummy and Daddy?"

"I NEED TO KNOW, MUMMY!!!"

then, 99 times out of a hundred (barring illness or a period of upheaval or the moon being in conjunction with Venus or whatever other mystical influences affecting children's sleep happen to come into play), we are able to come downstairs, get on with those important jobs we've been putting off all day (this is of course code for collapsing on the sofa to binge-watch crime dramas and eat Wagon Wheels) and get some well-earned rest before she barrels in at 6am shouting 'MORNING-CAN-WE-PLAY-GUESS-WHO-CAN-I-HAVE-A-DONUT-WHY-DON'T-ELEPHANTS-WEAR-HATS??' and other such soothing crack o'dawn streams of consciousness.

So, until then, just do what you need to do to get through it. If that means rocking them to sleep, crawling into bed with them, or throwing the towel in completely for the night and resigning yourself to another 2am cuddle session on the couch watching *Frozen*, so be it. Personally, I'm counting down the days until I can haul a grumpy teenager out of bed at 9am on a Sunday for a lovely family walk... BAHAHAHAHAHAHAHAAAAA!!!!

SEVEN

Health and safety

Some of you may have started this book hoping to pick up valuable hints, tips and tricks for raising small people. I can only imagine how disappointed you must be thus far. I'd like to say that it gets more useful and less sweary from here on in, but no such luck I'm afraid!

Anyway, let's talk health and safety. As the months roll by, toddler-proofing your house becomes one of the most important things on a parent's to-do list, am I right?

I mean, who DOESN'T want to protect all their best stuff, and themselves, from a 2-foot wrecking ball determined to destroy anything that isn't fortunate enough to be nailed down?

To that end, here are my 10 top tips for toddler-proofing your house:

1. When choosing a new sofa, not only consider how much you like it now, but whether it will be equally as appealing with a light coating of porridge, chocolate smears and the tears of the chronically sleep deprived.

2. **Password protect your phone!** It's unlikely anyone in your contact list wants to accept a video call and clap eyes on you taking a whizz whilst frantically screeching *"PUT MUMMY'S PHONE DOWN RIGHT NOW!"*, least of all your boss…

3. Having hot drinks around young children can potentially be very dangerous. Do you know what's not hot? Wine. #JustSaying

4. Use containers with child-resistant tops, but be aware that a clever toddler could undo them. Also be aware that your husband probably can't… if you're having a rough day, chuck his iPhone in one, call him, and prepare yourself for 10 whole minutes of laugh-out-loud fun!

5. Don't EVER leave your little one unattended. In fact, don't even blink. They live for that shit. Give them an inch and they'll take your keys, post them through the letter box and laugh their little heads off whilst you squeeze your ample behind through the living room window trying to retrieve them.

6. Use rubbish bins with childproof lids. Because **no one** enjoys playing 'find the wedding ring' in yesterday's chicken tikka masala.

7. Ensure your child's toys are not too heavy. That wooden bus may be aesthetically pleasing, but it will hurt like hell when the little fecker smacks you around the face with it…

8. Keep their cot well away from the windows. Yes, to avoid draughts, but *mainly* because you really don't need any passers-by witnessing the four-hour farce that is *"PLEASE JUST GO THE FUCKERTY-FUCK TO SLEEP!!"* every evening.

9. Remember that a visitor's bag could contain dangerous items or medication – so keep them out of reach. It's also worth considering just how pissed off said visitor will be in a week or so when they realise where that weird smell is coming from. (*I did wonder where the rest of her fish fingers went.*)

10. And finally, it's vital to have an escape plan in place for emergencies. Mine is sending Orla up to check on Daddy during one of his 40-minute "I'm just popping to the loo" episodes, then hotfooting it out the back door towards the local pub...

See? Sooooo many useful titbits for you there – you can thank me later.

In all seriousness though, as parents we will do everything humanly possible to avoid our children getting ill or injured, because their pain is our pain. And my God it's absolute carnage when one of those pesky sickness bugs worms its way into your household.

The timing is always absolutely impeccable, too. Partner away overnight? There's a 1000% chance of vom-o-clock for the unlucky sod left manning the fort. Got a wedding to go to? Be sure to pack the Calpol and whichever dress can best carry off an artistic streak of regurgitated vol-au-vents!

It's an actual mathematical equation – the more effort you put into planning the perfect outing / evening / getaway, the better your chances of everything unravelling in a haze of sneezes, shite and sweat roughly 20 minutes in.

Take our first family holiday, for example. Whilst every preparation was made to make it as child-friendly as possible, with a veritable smorgasbord of kiddie delights just a stone's throw away from our beautifully appointed holiday cottage, the truth is, kids (and viruses) don't give a monkey's that you're trying to make magical family memories here.

Let's relive some highlights.

As it was such a long drive, we 'wisely' decided to spend the night in a hotel en-route. This meant spending the first evening of our holiday sitting in silence in a blacked-out hotel room *from 6pm* so as not to wake the baby. Ever tried pouring wine into those tiny hotel bathroom glasses with just the light from your phone to guide you? It's a real skill…

The next day, approximately 30 minutes from our destination, she started making 'the face' and the car smelt like a skunk's arse. Next thing I know we've got a code-red poomaggeddon happening; it's pooling in the car seat, she's got her hands in it, absolute carnage. Time for a hasty pit-stop at the local service station, which, weirdly enough, appeared to be some kind of hotel as well. Orla was screaming blue murder on the changing table (which was of course only available in the ladies' toilets), so Jordan hovered awkwardly outside the door whilst I screamed for backup; "EVERYTHING is covered in shit; it's in her hair for fuck's sake! More wipes, MORE VESTS, GO-GO-GO!!!"

As we finally exited, I noticed that the room adjacent to the loos was hosting a very large (and unsurprisingly now rather subdued) pensioners' lunch. Dinner *and* a show, you lucky devils!

We eventually arrived and, after a thorough wet-wiping session and fresh change of clothes for all concerned, set off for the beach. Ahhhh, the beach – time to make life-long memories and share #blessed, sun-drenched selfies on Facebook.

She LOATHED the beach. The things she disliked most about it at that age included, but were by no means limited to: the sun, the sand, the sea, the breeze, and everybody else unfortunate enough to be there at the same time as us. We took the obligatory 'beach-fun' photo and left 15 minutes later. Truly a magical time!

Undeterred, we trekked dutifully through various parks, zoos, and cafes, capturing the odd smile here and there to show the folks back home what a lovely time we were having.

About half-way through the week, it transpired she was probably grumpier than usual for a very good reason – the vomiting virus she'd miraculously escaped at nursery had merely been lying in wait until we were all running on empty. I've genuinely never seen, or smelt, anything like it. At one point, every item of clothing we had was either soaking wet or covered in toddler-vom, giving choosing what to wear of a morning all the appeal of deciding which Chuckle Brother I'd rather snog.

Do you know what would make this holiday even better, I thought? If we could stay up ALL NIGHT! As sure as night follows day, as her temperature rose, her sleep routine went completely and utterly to shit. Cue hours of bleary-eyed despair whilst watching endless *In the Night Garden* episodes. If I'd wanted to spend my summer with a truckload of oddbods riding in circles around the countryside, I'd have taken a sodding coach trip…

So yes, all in all, an absolute riot.

To be fair, by the end of the week she'd recovered and settled in sufficiently to actually enjoy herself, and those are days I look back on really fondly. But bloody hell, it was hard work.

The poorly days do certainly give you a renewed appreciation for the ordinary ones, though. Turns out you can handle pretty much anything they throw at you as long as it's not the insides of an under 5…

A final, vital note on the subject of illness is that, once you have kids, you are rarely offered the luxury of being allowed to be ill yourself. Which a bit of a pain in the arse given how frequently your little germ muffins will sneeze into your eyeballs or poke their mud-encrusted fingers down your throat just for shits and giggles.

Case in point, here's another lovely parenting fairy story to wind up this chapter.

The Lie Down

Once upon a time, Mummy went for a little lie down.

This was partly because she was feeling ill, and partly because the thought of sitting through yet another 'Oooh-Tube' video of Blippi twatting about in a ball pit made her want to chew her own arm off and throw it at him. So off she went.

The very second Mummy's head touched the pillow, Daddy wandered in to check if she'd seen his wallet. He had looked everywhere, he said. Mummy knew that this statement was bullshittery of the highest order. Five seconds later, having found said wallet expertly hidden in the lost city of 'on the kitchen side, clear as day, where it always bloody is', Mummy hauled herself back into bed, and closed her eyes.

Roughly one millisecond had passed when:

"Mummy?? Can I have a ham sandwich?"

Mummy decided to blow her small person's mind with the revelation that Daddy was A), also tall enough to reach the fridge and B), familiar with the recipe, and sent her on her merry way.

Finally! Time to slee…

"MUMMY!!!! I banged my head!!!"

Oh Christ…

"*Quick, let me look at you! Are you ok baby, where does it hurt? What did you bang it on?*"

"*George.*"

"*… George?*"

"*George.*"

"*George as in George your friend from nursery? George as in George who you've been nowhere near in 4 days? THAT fecking George?*"

"*… Yes.*"

"*So this in fact happened… last week?*"

"*… Yes. Want to play Hungry Hippos?*"

Walking wounded swiftly dispatched back downstairs, Mummy took a moment to drink in the glorious silence and drifted off.

Approximately 20 seconds later, Mummy sensed that someone else was in the room with her. (I say 'sensed': it's fairly difficult to ignore someone prising your eyelids open and screaming "*ARE YOU ASLEEP MUMMY?*" directly into your eye sockets.)

Apparently, Mummy had selfishly chosen to nap in the exact same spot where the Stuffed Animal Olympics were scheduled to kick off. "*Don't worry Mummy, we're just going to do QUIET jumping.*"

Fan-bloody-tastic.

Mummy finally accepted the futility of it all and headed downstairs, clearly so visibly re-energised by her third-of-a-minute of shut-eye that her husband remarked, "*Feeling better now? Mind if I have 30 minutes?*"

The End

Loved this classic tale? Don't miss the thrilling sequel: 'Party in the Bathroom – Mummy's Having a Wee!'

EIGHT

Off to work we go

I went back to work when Orla was about 5 months old (the main reason being that statutory maternity pay is terrible and we burned through our savings with terrifying ease).

I'm always a bit hesitant to describe myself as a 'working mother', for fear it implies that I think stay-at-home mothers are not working, when I know all too well that being in charge of tiny hoodlums all day is by far the hardest job of all!

In fact, as much as I miss my little girl and look forward to the days that I get to spend with her, there are certain aspects of the work environment that I have a *whole* new appreciation for since becoming a mother:

- When I want to go to the toilet, nobody insists on accompanying me. And if there's no loo roll, it's because the previous occupant's been a lazy bollox, not because someone's now standing *just* out of reach, clutching it in their tiny mitts and grinning like a deranged supervillain – "*QUITE the pickle you've gotten yourself into here, mama…*"

- It's sooooo bloomin' lovely and clean there! No Fisher-Price obstacle course to navigate every time you leave the room, no nagging fear whenever you move something that a family of abandoned turkey dinosaurs might be lurking underneath it… and I have *never once* stood in the tea room contemplating whether to drink my coffee out of a sippy cup rather than tackle the mountain of washing up.

- Lunchtime is, believe it or not, a period during which food is actually consumed! At home, Orla spends roughly 30% of that time pissing about with her peas, 40% lobbing the rest of it across the room, and the remainder chewing on one of her highchair straps, which apparently taste far nicer than anything I can concoct in the kitchen. These days, everyone's a critic…

- Sometimes, you have to say no to your colleagues – generally they take this on the chin and find an alternative solution. On no occasion have they reacted by having a shit-fit on the carpet or lunging at me with a spatula. (*Is anyone else's child unhealthily attached to their kitchen utensils?*)

- Most importantly – thus far, not one of my co-workers has asked me to wiggle my bottom, spin around or save the day with the mystical power of aerobics (**feck OFF**, Tree Fu Tom!)

On a slightly more serious note, I think the fundamental reason work doesn't always feel as much like, well, *work* as being at home can, is that the stakes aren't nearly as high. I love my job, but how well I do it doesn't affect whether lives are saved, or great injustices are righted. Whereas at home, there's that ever-present nagging feeling that every choice I make, every mistake (and there are a LOT of those), could impact on my daughter's development or future happiness.

At home, it's just us. No one else can make the hard calls or pitch in and help with the toughest jobs. Equally, there's no annual appraisal to review all the good work you've done that year, no promotion or pay rise, no public 'thumbs up' on the company blog – you just have to keep on trucking, through the good days and the bad.

But, in my heart of hearts, when I'm able to step back a bit from the non-stop chaos, I KNOW I'm doing an OK job. She certainly seems to think so; either that or she's kept her recruitment drive for my replacement pretty damn quiet…

THE BIG QUESTION when returning to work is of course who is going to tag-team the childcare situation. Family, childminder, nursery? In the end, after a few very lucky initial months when my mum was able to do the lion's share as I settled back in, we decided on nursery. Although eye-wateringly expensive (we did some serious happy dancing the day her 3-year funding kicked in), it has turned out to be an amazing experience for her.

It's hard to pinpoint what makes one childcare setting stand out from the rest when you're looking around, but I think a lot of it comes down to 'the feeling' you get. Aside from lots of great recommendations, we loved that the nursery we chose let you come and look around at any time rather than having to turn up for a specific tour – they were happy that you would get a good impression of them whenever you chose to rock up. They had a few different rooms for the babies for sleepy time, messy time, sensory time etc., which I really liked as many facilities seemed to just have the one small room for the youngest group. And most of all, in every room, children seemed completely at ease, boisterous and laughing – the staff themselves were getting completely stuck in and were absolutely covered in paint and glitter. It seemed like a really joyous and relaxed place to be.

That's not to say the transition period wasn't tough, for both of us. It's a really big deal handing your baby over to someone else for the day. The first time I dropped her off, I went back to the car and cried my eyes out. But within a couple of weeks, Orla had developed an amazing bond with her keyworker, Miss Adele – if we came across a photo of the two of them on my phone, her face lit up and she would cover the screen with kisses. When I went to collect her in the evening and took a peek through the window (it's soooo strange catching a glimpse of this whole other world of theirs that you're not a part of) I could see her giggling away as she played, or babbling excitedly about a toy she'd discovered, and I knew she was OK there without me.

More than OK, actually – I'm always a little mystified by what they manage to get her to do there!

At the end of each day, I get sent a little report on what she's been up to, which seems to be fairly standard practice these days. Does anybody else read these and worry they've mixed your child up with another, less feral, classmate?

Here are some examples, with my 'mum report' extracts for comparison (thank God we don't actually have to submit one of these; I'd have Ofsted banging on my door within the week).

Storytime

Nursery: *Orla loved looking at different storybooks with Miss Adele, pointing at the different pictures, feeling the textures and changing pages one by one.*

Home: Orla insisted on reading *Fox's Socks* 35 fun-filled times this morning, which made Mummy wonder how Mr Fox would fare without other, more vital appendages… Orla also enjoyed ripping the flaps out of the book one by one, which should really speed up the sock-finding process next time around…

Playtime

Nursery: *Orla loved engaging with the wooden and metal heuristic toys and attempting to correctly place hoops on the sticks.*

Home: Orla *adored* jamming Mummy's wooden spoon into the DVD player; Mummy was much less keen on this. Mummy said a bad word when the frying pan Orla was wielding engaged with her kneecap. Orla had a complete shit-fit when the round shape refused to fit through the square hole in her shape sorter. She also thinks Mummy is an arsehole for not being able to bend the laws of physics and make this possible. Mummy has put the shape sorter in a 'safe place' whilst everyone calms down.

Nursery lunchtime

 11:30 AM to 12:00 PM - fish goujons with new potatoes, lime and mint puree - eaten all

 11:30 AM to 12:00 PM - cocoa, date & coconut pudding - eaten all

(As an aside here, bloody hell! This looks SO much more appealing than my lunchbox – do you think they deliver?)

Lunchtime with me

11:30am: healthy lunch option that Mummy has put her blood, sweat and tears into making – eaten sweet FA!!

12:00pm: Mummy gives up and falls back on that old favourite, 50 shades of beige, adding some fruit she knows won't get eaten just to make herself feel better…

Naptime

z^zZ   12:05 PM to 02:30PM -

This is the bit that *really* gets my goat. Somehow, those magical nursery pixies manage to get 10+ under 2s to all lie down on mats AT THE SAME TIME and just go to sleep! For hours! What the actual fuck? Are they all so full after their Michelin-starred, perfectly balanced lunch that they just have to sleep it off immediately? I've only got one child to worry about and I'm still driving her aimlessly around the village every lunchtime singing 'Baa Baa Black Sheep' until she finally gives in.

Music time

Nursery: *Orla enjoyed playing with the musical instruments at group time this afternoon, smiling and babbling away.*

Home: Mummy put a wash on this afternoon and was rather bemused to find that it was jangling. Orla watched her tambourine go round and round in the washing machine, smiling and babbling away, as Mummy stomped off to call Daddy and share the delightful day she was having.

End of day

Nursery: *Orla was picked up by her father.*

Home: Orla was picked up by her mother and thrown at her father the minute he set foot inside the door.

Would it be weird if I asked Miss Adele to come on holiday with us this year? I think it might be a bit more relaxing if we take the child *she* gets to look after every day.

. . .

TOP TIP: There are so many ways these days to treasure the works of art that your child creates for you every 30 seconds or so at nursery. You could make a collage / talking point for your living room wall, snap a picture and upload them all into a snazzy online portfolio, or even turn them into unique wallpaper destined to take pride of place in your home for decades to come.

OR – you could chuck them all in your car boot, because TECHNICALLY you haven't thrown them away, and it's going to be years before she's tall enough to look in there and find you out...

SO, I guess what I'm trying to say is, the thought of going back to work after having a child can be really daunting, with a big dollop of good-old mum guilt that you'll no longer be spending every minute with them. But in my experience, Orla has completely thrived at nursery, and I have actually enjoyed getting a piece of myself back for a few hours a day when I can talk to other grownups and remind myself that I still have plenty to offer the world as Siobhan, not just 'mum'. Not that there aren't days when I'm completely wiped out by juggling pick-ups and drop-offs with strategy meetings and product launches, not to mention having that "oh **bugger**! It's World Book Day / World Mud Day / World-Catch-Parents-Out-With-Farfetched-National-Holiday-Requiring-An-Elaborate-Costume-and-Craft-Day" moment at least once a week!

I'M GOING to finish this chapter with one of our nursery highlights / lowlights – that Friday evening when you stroll up to the front door to pick up your little darling, only to hear the words you've been dreading for months now.

Yup – we'd been landed with the sodding Class Bear for the bank holiday weekend. Bertie arrived with enough luggage for a fortnight in the Bahamas and a diary jam-packed with exciting and exotic adventures that previous children had embarked on with their intrepid little explorer. Meanwhile, I had nothing remotely interesting planned for the weekend other than a trip to the local farm and a whizz around Aldi.

Anyway, if you're wondering how he got on, Bertie put together a lovely little photo journal for you to read.

It *really* goes without saying that this isn't the draft I sent over to nursery!

My Weekend

By Bertie the Class Bear

Who the f*ck packed my luggage? No alcohol,
no snacks, ONE outfit for three whole days and,
inexplicably, this cock and balls spoon...

"PSST! Is the food always this bad here? Why's
everything beige? I DEMAND to speak to the
chef! Tell Captain Birdseye to get his arse over
here pronto..."

She did WHAT with his throbbing member?
Blimey, you don't get this kind of action in *The
Very Hungry Caterpillar*…

"Look, all I'm saying is that Mr Tumble and
Justin look PRETTY fookin similar…"

"You serious, lads? Aldi?? The last kid took me to Alton Towers! And Barbara, SLOW the F*CK down, this isn't Supermarket Sweep. I just got nutted by a packet of custard creams travelling at 90 miles an hour…"

Me thinks that Peter Rabbit needs to ease up on the Domino's a bit… #NeverMeetYourHeroes

And I thought I was having a shit holiday…

I mean, who DOESN'T enjoy being drop kicked
down a slide by a toddler?

FML. Seriously, FMAL. I bet Winnie the Pooh
doesn't have to put up with this shite…

♪"99 buckets of sand up my arse, 99 buckets of SAND…"♪ #LivingMyBestLife

"Dafuq you looking at ass-hat??"

"Yeah, you BETTER run! Bloody llamas strutting about like they own the place…"

Apparently, my 'Bertie-Big-Bollocks fuckwittery' at the farm was not appreciated, so I'm doing some serious thinking about my behaviour in this weird multi-storey perspex prison. Not sure why I'm naked, though. Probably doesn't bode well…

Kids are in bed, sun's shining... time for a cheeky glass of vino. Well, one more couldn't hurt...

hiccup and sometimes I just think… "Bertie, what's the bloody POINT?? They take you home on Friday and it's all 'Oooh Bertie sit with me, play with me, sleep in my bed!' Come Monday, they hand over the diary and just f*ck off to the home corner. "Bertie WHO, Mummy??" BEARS HAVE FEELINGS TOO, YOU LITTLE FECKERS!

Something tells me he won't be rushing back for a return visit anytime soon…

NINE

The terrible twos

Don't you just know it when you have a two-year-old?

The rage, the tears, that perpetual scowl that screams *"WHY ARE YOU RUINING MY LIFE?!"* (and of course, plenty of *actual* screaming; she nearly deafened me yesterday when I suggested that her father's pants weren't appropriate headgear for nursery).

I have to ask, my gorgeous-most, stroppy-most one; is it REALLY so terrible being two?

Here are a few reasons why I think you should reconsider your 'everything sucks' stance on toddler life:

Naps

Why on earth would you refuse a nap?? I would LOVE a nap right now!

You have a team of people on hand trying every trick in the book to coax you to sleep, then when you wake up, we congratulate **YOU** for doing so well! When you're a parent there is *noooooo* such thing as a free nap. If one of you lets the other take an impromptu snooze, the napper will spend the remainder of the day on edge, waiting for some God-awful poonami / tantrum / Teletubby-down-the-toilet incident to occur, just KNOWING that the next thing they hear will be "*Well, you DID get to have that extra kip earlier*". Right-oh – I'm off to rescue Tinky-sodding-Winky from the bog, then…

You are the champion. All the time.

And I hate to break it to you kid, but *whispers*: *We're letting you win!!*

I know this is a rather rude awakening for you, but I'm not actually THAT shit at football, or running, or Hide and Seek (FYI – the seeking part is made slightly less tricky when you merely shuffle two steps to the left of me, put your hands over your eyes and shout '*gone!*').

Zero social obligations

Adults can't just leave social events they're not enjoying – we're obliged to make awkward small talk, wait it out until the first person exits, then hightail it out of there immediately afterwards and bitch all the way home about those four hours of our lives we'll never get back. It's the law.

You, however, can toddle into the room, quickly assess that it's not your scene, pull your dress up over your face and weep piteously until someone gives in and escorts you from the premises. In all fairness, if I tried that, I'd probably get to leave a lot earlier too…

We do all the worrying for you

It may **FEEL** like I'm being a total buzzkill when I won't let you play with my phone in the bath, or climb into the bin, or bring that dog poo you found at the park home to show Daddy… but one day, when you're all grown up, you might actually miss having someone on hand to step in and stop you making bad choices. For example, I could have REALLY done with this a decade or so ago when I attended a Halloween-themed boat party dressed as a pirate and drank SO MUCH RUM that I ended up getting into a slanging match with Wonder Woman, tripping over my own sword and vomiting into the Thames… #rumisNOTyourfriend

Dramatic, much?

I know it's crap when another kid takes your ball at softplay, but let's get a bit of perspective here… you are currently standing **IN A BALL PIT**, surrounded by literally hundreds of the bloody things, which I can guarantee you are each as identically unhygienic as the last. It's really not the end of the world.

You just wait until you're all grown up and some absolute wank puffin at work methodically works their way through YOUR BUTTER (which has your name on it and everything; this isn't amateur hour) leaving you stuck with that rancid *'I can totally believe it's not butter – it's shite'* nonsense lurking at the back of the fridge. That, my girl, is a real fecking liberty…

ANYWAY, being two is a big deal. The milestones just seem to keep on coming: actual sentences, imaginative play, being able to climb up and down absolutely everything in the house without help (got to be honest, that's not my favourite one).

RECENTLY, our Health Visitor Amanda came a-calling for Orla's 2-year check. If you have one coming up, here are my 10 takeaways from the experience:

1. Despite knowing this was a standard check on my child's progress and not an examination of my parenting skills, 5 minutes before she arrived, I found myself casually laying out bowls of fruit and putting the CBeebies ballet on in a last-ditch attempt to look like I had my shit together (and cover up Orla's chronic addiction to Paw Patrol and custard creams).

2. If you're going to go to all the trouble of 'setting the scene' this way, it helps if you remember that an entire Christmas holiday's worth of empty wine bottles are currently sitting in the recycling box outside your front door. Totally aced that first impression!

3. Any other day of the week your child will confidently point to a picture of a car, or tell you what noise a dog makes, but they can somehow sense that their answer is marginally more important this time around and will therefore point-blank refuse to play ball. (Unbelievably, you get no extra points for enthusiastically woofing at the Health Visitor yourself).

4. Having confiscated certain items pre-visit, I spent the majority of the time whipping new

dummies out of her mouth, which she seemed to be pulling out of thin air ("*Oh yes, she only EVER has them at night*") and trying to convince Amanda she was saying 'rabbit' when she was actually demanding my tablet (Damn you YouTube with your magic child-whispering voodoo).

5. If, like me, you somehow managed to mislay the form before the appointment (whoops), you may be somewhat taken aback by the nature of the questions. I'm sorry, Amanda, but I'm really not sure if my child can successfully extract a single raisin from a clear plastic bottle, or build a scale model of the Taj Mahal using only lollipop sticks and fromage frais… I thought this was a development check, not The Crystal Maze! And some of the tasks seem way too advanced. I mean, "*Does your child put things away where they belong?*" My husband is in his thirties and still hasn't cracked that.

6. Surely "*Do you have any concerns about your child's behaviour?*" is a trick question?

7. Turns out I've been chastising Orla for activities that are **actually** key milestones: "*Does your child flip switches off and on?*" All the bloody time! Who doesn't enjoy a quick game of Finger Russian Roulette when you're busy chopping vegetables and repeatedly being plunged into darkness? "*If your child wants something she cannot reach, does she find a chair or box to stand on to reach it?*" Honest to God, at the very moment she asked the question, I glanced to my left and saw Orla standing on her little IKEA chair gleefully helping herself to the biscuit tin – tick!

8. Sometimes, it's best not to go into too much detail with your answers. For example, when asked if Orla regularly copies the activities I do, I decided to go with a brief *"oh yes, definitely"*, inwardly cringing over the time I found her busily making dinner at her toy kitchen whilst muttering 'God's sake' into her toy phone… it was like looking into my own, judgemental little mirror…

9. Try not to take too much offence if the child who normally greets strangers with nothing less than open hostility insists that the Health Visitor stays to play, blows her kisses and cries when she leaves (*"Bye then Amanda,* **SHE LOVES IT HERE REALLY!***"*)

10. And finally, I've decided not to lose any sleep over the fact that Orla was unable to identify the miniscule drawing she was presented with. Here's a fairly accurate recreation:

WTF **is** that, Amanda?!? A person? A snowman? A one-legged cat with a pitchfork? Pictionary is clearly not your forte…

ANOTHER BIG CHANGE we experienced from age two was a sudden and overwhelming 'couldn't possibly eat / sleep / take-another-step-without-them' attachment to cuddly toys.

Let me introduce you to Mama Spot *(so called because she comes in a set with a smaller puppy who we named, you guessed it, Spot... we are so flipping creative in this household).*

Up until now, Orla barely even glanced at the lovely cuddlies that well-meaning family members trotted in with at birthdays and Christmases. Her previous sidekicks of choice included a baking potato and a tape measure.

But then came Mama Spot. She goes to bed with her, in the car with her, even to nursery, where she sits in her own special basket to keep an eye on her for us.

I am now genuinely terrified that something might happen to Mama Spot. I actually had a nightmare last night that I couldn't find her – it was horrific. What has my life come to? *

I'd like to swoop in from the future at this point, dear reader, and let you know that we did in fact lose Mama Spot. Many, many times. I say 'we'; I am of course referring to butterfingers magoo herself – the 2-foot terror with the attention span of a gnat and a penchant for 'hiding' her most treasured possession, only to lose all memory of doing so approximately three-quarters of a second later.

So, I hope you enjoy my version of 'We're Going on a Bear Hunt' – dedicated to every parent who has experienced that heart-stopping moment when their child's cuddly bestie suddenly goes AWOL.

The Bear Hunt

We're goin' on a bear hunt
(She'll never sleep without it)
Why didn't we buy a spare one??
(YOU said we didn't need one!)
But we're not scared!
(We're really shit-scared)
Where the fuck could he be?
*(Where **THE FUCK** could he be?!?)*
MAYBE we left him in Aldi…

Uh-uh! The Middle Aisle!
The chock-a-bloc, odd-o'clock Middle Aisle
We can't go over it.
We can't go under it.

Oh no!
We've got to go through it!
Oooh look – a lawnmower!
(We haven't got time for this…)
I've always wanted a popcorn maker!
(Put that down or you'll meet your maker…)
A pet crate!
(FFS!)
BALLS *– no sign of the bloody bear.*
MAYBE we left him at softplay…

Uh-uh! A ball pit!
A deep, dark, hygienically-questionable ball pit.
We can't go over it.
We can't go under it.
Oh no!
We've got to go through it!
Squelch squerch!
(This bear's SUCH a cock)
Squelch squerch!
(Something's stuck to my sock!!)
Squelch squerch!
Which ABSOLUTE chump
Left their half-eaten Flump
In this grotty, snotty ball pit??
BOLLOCKS *– no sign of the bloody bear.*
MAYBE we left him at Pets at Home…

Uh-uh! Rabbits!
Cutsie, cuddlesome, "I REALLY REALLY
*   WANT ONE MUM!!" rabbits.*
We can't go over them.
We can't go under them.
We've got to go through them!

"PLEAAAASE – JUST ONE!"

(It'll cost us a bomb!)

"PLEAAASE – I'll LOOK AFTER IT!"

(It'll shit on the carpet!)

"BUT I NEEEEED ONE, THOUGH!"

For the last time, NO!!!

Sod it, let's just go home…

WAIT!

WHAT'S THAT IN THE BOOT OF THE CAR??

One shiny nose!

Two big furry ears!

Two big goggly eyes!

IT'S BEAR!

*You have **GOT** to be fucking kidding me…*

Quick!

Drive home.

Open the door.

Up the stairs.

BEDTIME!

Phew.

Right then –

I'm goin' on a wine hunt…

TEN

The wonderful world of children's entertainment

One of the things I was really looking forward to about having a child was sharing my love of reading with them. What I failed to realise was that before we get to the bit where we can snuggle up at bedtime with *The Secret Garden* and *Charlotte's Web*, there's THIS bit, where we have to read about dogs losing balls and sheep that are crap at hiding. Over and over again. *Every* bloomin' day.

Let me walk you through Orla's current faves:

Fox's Socks

Charming – the first 20 times you read it. Now I'm really starting to lose patience with this guy.

No wonder you can't find them – it's a bloody tip in there! Spend a little less time rhyming and a little more picking up after yourself and we won't have to go through this sodding charade every day. And who only has one pair of socks, anyway? You're living in a prime piece of real estate full of antique furniture, with some kind of live-in

mouse-maid tending to your every whim – surely you can stretch to a second pair?

And I'm sorry, but look at that alarm clock… I have absolutely no sympathy for someone who gets to sleep in until 10am.

Dear Zoo

If you've not had the pleasure, *Dear Zoo* is about a kid who bypasses Pets At Home and instigates some kind of 'try before you buy' scheme with his local zoo.

So, they send over an elephant in a really solid-looking crate, a lion in a metal cage labelled 'Danger!', then a ginormous fecking snake… IN A WICKER BASKET! No warning sign, no '*I'd think twice before putting your hand in there, fella*', nothing. Perhaps the staff were getting a bit sick of the whole enterprise by then and hoped for a swift, if brutal, end to the entire affair – I imagine the postage alone was costing a fortune.

In the Night Garden: Everybody Loves Christmas!

As you will find out very shortly in the CBeebies section of this chapter, we have a bit of a love / hate relationship in our household with this motley crew. *(Orla LOVES them, I think the world would be a much better place if they all climbed*

aboard the Pinky Ponk and sodded off somewhere else.)

In addition to spending every evening with them, I also get to scrape Igglepiggle stickers off the furniture every morning, stage elaborate dramas with the figurines, and read this festive classic countless times a day. In June.

Let's just take a moment to try and work out what on earth is HAPPENING here??

Are they being held up by the Feds? Bowing to their cult leader? Something else that shifty-looking characters get up to in deserted parks at midnight? I try not to think about it too much…

That's not my... unicorn / badger / panda / Tequila

I don't think it's possible to be a parent these days and not have at least three of these lying about the place. A couple of them have given me cause for concern, though:

That's not my baby – its mittens are too fuzzy – if you can't pick your own child out of a line-up without giving their gloves a quick once-over, you are going to be completely fucked when summer rolls around.

And this particular page…

Back away mate, you're spending *way* too much quality time with your livestock (and don't even get me started on what that creepy little mouse is up to).

The Very Hungry Caterpillar

In fairness, I haven't got a bad word to say about this absolute legend. Once upon a time, someone stuffed their face with junk food, slept for a fortnight, and woke up feeling GORGEOUS. That's the kind of positive affirmation of my lifestyle preferences that I'm looking for in a lead character…

·   ·   ·

BUT HEY, it's all reading right, with plenty of valuable cognitive and imaginative development happening somewhere along the line.

Slightly more dubious in terms of its educational contribution, but none the less essential for five minutes of peace and the occasional hot drink, is the wonderful world of kids' TV – a murky whirlpool of primary colours, perky presenters and shouty jingles that we have inevitably been sucked further and further into as the years have progressed.

Once upon a time, Jordan and I were relatively normal people who discussed the grown-up television issues of the day, like who made the best Dampfnudel in this week's *Bake Off*, or when winter would finally get the fuck on with it and arrive in *Game of Thrones*.

Now that CBeebies has become the soundtrack of our lives, the true marker of time (it's going to be a looonnng bloody day if you're up pre-Chris and Pui), we find ourselves analysing the ins and outs of its offerings far too frequently…

Postman Pat and the P45

The man has the cushiest gig going – six, maybe seven people to deliver letters to, tops, plus the odd special delivery to the local school. Yet he is never, ever on time. Not even close. What's worse is that the villagers have become completely conditioned to it! Whilst Pat gallivants across the hills chasing the latest victim of his ineptitude, some poor sap checks their watch and sighs, "*It's not like Pat to be late.*"

YES IT FECKING IS!!! Where have you *been* the last three series? Open your eyes, Mrs Goggins!

My best guess as to why he's still gainfully employed is

that anyone else with the very specific helicopter, light aircraft and boat licences required by the Greendale postal service these days has found a slightly more lucrative position.

Raa Raa, you are... a bit of a bellend

My main beef with Raa Raa is the absolute sadist who decided that the best time to schedule jingly-jangly ear-splitting fun in the jungle was **6.45am**! What is required at this hour is coffee and calming voices, not some noisy little knobgoblin roaring at anything that looks sideways at him.

Murdering wildlife - it's a Bing thing

It feels like I've missed the all-important pilot episode of Bing which explains how a menagerie of talking baby animals came to be looked after by bean-bag people half their size. The houses and furniture are adult-animal-sized, so where are they all? My sister's theory is that it's some kind of hostile alien takeover and this is the part where the new alien leaders subtly brainwash the young to accept the new world order.

It's clearly affecting Bing, whose crimes are escalating daily – stealing, mindless vandalism, butterfly murdering… but luckily, nothing ever phases the unflappable Flop. Although I like to think he spends at least some of his time screaming silently into the fridge before trudging off to clean up Bing's latest mishap.

Topsy and Tim - where the fun never begins

Genuinely interested to know who is actually watching this? I can't imagine that any child is actually sitting there, mouth agape, hoping against hope that Mr Rosen's wheelie bag arrives in time for his weekly shop, or punching the air in delight when Daddy Odell finally finishes the swing set he's spent the entire episode screwing together.

It is however entirely possible that my dislike of this programme stems from the perfectly groomed Mrs Odell making me feel like a totally inadequate mother. The wrapping paper hasn't arrived for Kerry's birthday present? No problem twins, let's head over to our designated crafting area and whip up some home-made stuff! Nursery's had to close for the day? OF COURSE I don't mind if the entire class spends the day at our house covering every available surface in poster paint and Monster Munch! Oh do sod off, Joy…

Trapped in the Night Garden

We made the rookie error of incorporating *In the Night Garden* into the bedtime routine, so for fear of jinxing the whole sleeping through thing, we now have to sit through 28 minutes of Igglepiggle and co. EVERY NIGHT. Given that a little piece of me dies every time Makka Pakka trundles over looking for Tombliboos to sponge down, I think that the least they could do is put a bit of effort into sorting out the blindingly obvious scale issues. The ball CANNOT be the same size as the Pinky Ponk and yet small enough to be held by someone who fits inside the Pinky Ponk. It's just not possible. Sort it out, guys!

Please tell me it's not just me lying awake at night trying to figure all this out?

ALL THIS SETS you on the very slippery slope towards remortgaging your house to afford those must-have toys, cuddlies, lunchboxes, pyjamas and magazines plastered with Bing and co.'s annoying little mugs, culminating in an entire day expressly designed to part parents from both their money and their sanity – the official theme park experience.

Yes, I'm talking about that parental realm of eternal pain and suffering also known as CBeebies Land.

I'm going to preface the following with the undeniable fact that Orla absolutely loved it, and asked if we could go again tomorrow the entire way home *(hell-to-the-no, my lovely)*.

Anyhoo, here are our key takeaways if you too are a glutton for punishment looking to drop a small fortune on branded tat, warm sandwiches and, of course, creating magical family memories…

- Upon exiting the car park, if your partner says "THE MONORAIL? But it's a LOVELY day! And we'll be waiting for AGES! It's *only* a short walk!" you are completely within your rights to continuously berate him *(quietly, because there may be kids present who aren't as familiar with terms like 'twunt' and 'cock womble' as your own family)* for the entire 5-mile hike to the entrance. Whilst pushing a ridiculously heavy buggy. In 27-degree heat. Totally over it now, BTW…

- When you cross the threshold, small child fizzing with excitement and anticipation, and ask them who they'd like to see first, and they say "PAW PATROL!!! NO, BLAZE!!! NO, PEPPA!!!" this is a strong indicator that you've completely mismanaged the outing explanation and will very shortly be paying for it in tears and copious amounts of CCC (crisis consolation chocolate).

- Speaking of which, bring queue snacks. ALL THE QUEUE SNACKS. I met at least four other parents who were on their second day in the park, having stayed overnight, and this was literally the first thing they would say, in the kind of urgent tone a survivor might use to impart life-saving advice a couple of days into an apocalypse. One particularly frazzled-looking mum admitted to raiding the hotel breakfast bar that morning and loading her husband up like some kind of illicit snack mule after a soul-destroying tantrum in the Go Jetters queue the previous day when she ran out of Pringles...

- A real highlight of the trip is that I think we've FINALLY cured Orla of her Bing obsession. Turning a corner to find an 8-foot sweaty rabbit lumbering with intent towards her really seems to have done the trick!

- You know that bit at the end of a ride when you trundle off to the photo booth and try not to recoil in horror as you, The Grimace Family, pop up between the picture-perfect snaps of other children smiling adorably, and mums who miraculously still have perfect lip gloss and flicky hair despite being on a bloody rollercoaster? I feel like if you then say, "God no, I'm not paying a tenner for that!" the guy behind the counter should read the room a bit better and not counter with something along the lines of "Ahh, but for the price of a week in the Maldives you can have it IN A KEYRING!!!" Flipping fantastic, Jake, where do I sign?

- You cannot fool the ride attendants into thinking your son is taller than 0.9 metres by precariously balancing his baseball cap on top of his hair and hoping for the best. But I have to commend the guy in front of us in the Justin's House queue for giving it a good crack.

- Surrounded by dozens of flashy, interactive, thrills-and-spills-a-plenty rides, Orla's absolute favourite place was Charlie & Lola's House, which was in essence a ball pit and a tunnel. So yes, we'd essentially travelled 80+ miles at stupid o'clock in the morning to do the exact same thing she could have done in the softplay centre around the corner...

- Although *In the Night Garden* is a complete head-fuck, it still made me SO HAPPY when I heard that theme tune every night because, afterwards, it meant BEDTIME. And SITTING DOWN. And GROWN-UP TIME. Well, those absolute monsters at Alton Towers have completely ruined it by putting the only exit from the Night Garden boat ride DIRECTLY THROUGH THE GIFT SHOP! You can't go over it, you can't go under it, (*you certainly can't fob your child off with that lie about gift shops being closed on Mondays now*), you HAVE to go through it! We finally made it out with a sticker book and a cuddly talking veggie from Mr Bloom and counted ourselves lucky. £10 for a sodding runner bean! I don't think anyone's been shafted this badly by a guy selling beans since Jack and his beanstalk!

Will we end up there again? Almost certainly. Will we ever manage to get a decent photo of us living the #blessed #makingmemories #familyfun life? Unlikely, given the evidence below, which I can assure you was the very best photo of the day...

ELEVEN

Out and about

I've just rolled in from another action-packed softplay session and realised that the whole experience is a real throwback to the bygone era of my student days: the sticky floors, the dated tunes blaring out at a volume that makes your ears bleed, that faint whiff of vomit...

Here's why softplay is a lot like going clubbing:

- The name of the place is usually a bit off-the-wall and hints at the carnage that will ensue inside: *Pandemonium, Kidzmania, Berserk* – my absolute favourite is the unwittingly evocative *Ding Dong Fun Bus* in London, which sounds more like something the Chippendales would tour on...

- It's massively overpriced – an extortionate entry fee, luke-warm drinks; but they have you over a barrel because nowhere else is open at this ungodly hour!

- It's wall-to-wall sweaty people – 50% of whom look like they'd rather be literally anywhere else.

- Someone's definitely pissed all over the toilet floor.

- You can spot the birthday crew a mile off – they're hogging all the tables, incredibly over-excited, and at least one of them is wearing a Superhero costume.

- There's a girl openly sobbing in the corner because she's fallen out with all her mates.

- In the opposite corner, there's a lad who's already sleeping it off, despite the fact that he only walked in 30 minutes ago. Before you know it, he'll be throwing up in the loos and staggering about the place on his second wind…

- You'll hugely overestimate how steady you are on your feet, and invariably end up falling on your arse and trying not to cry.

- There's always that one guy making a complete prat of himself and ruining it for everyone else (this week it happened to be my husband, who forgot that he was by far the heaviest occupant of the bouncy castle zone and bounced a little TOO enthusiastically; the whole thing dipped and about 20 kids hit the deck and rolled into him).

- An hour or so in, you're really keen to go, but the annoying person you came with keeps running off and absolutely refuses to leave because they're having *"THE BEST TIME EVERRRRRR!"*

- You finally escape – bruised, bedraggled and absolutely knackered, vowing never to cross the threshold again (whilst knowing you'll almost certainly be back next week).

I don't know about you but since becoming parents, we seem to spend about 50% of our lives in some kind of padded horror zone like the above, or chucking food pellets at distinctly unimpressed barnyard animals. Remember when a stamp on your hand signified an epic night of cocktails and dancing? Now it means you've signed up for a fun-packed morning traipsing around yet another bloody farm in the pouring rain, getting slobbered on by goats and spending a month's wages on sausage rolls...

OF COURSE, you don't need to spend a fortune on expensive days out; there are plenty of places where your offspring can royally twunt about in full view of unsuspecting members of the public that don't even charge.

Take the supermarket shop, for example. As a rule, we do our weekly shop online – man delivers 30 items in 30 different shopping bags, Orla upends anything she can get hold of onto the doormat and hurls a couple of onions under the sofa, I stab frantically at that electronic pad thing and scrawl something that looks nothing like my signature so that I can finally shut the door on the utter destruction unfolding within – job done!

However, sometimes (OK, often) it completely slips my mind to actually place the order during the 24/7 mothering juggling act that is now life, which means dedicating an entire morning to surviving the supermarket with an under 5 in tow.

New to this? Here are some tried-and-tested strategies for getting in and out in one piece (ideally with at least half of the things that you meant to buy).

Firstly, you'll need to grow a thick skin, because if children see an opening to show you up in front of complete strangers, they will *definitely* take it, and any pensioners in the immediate vicinity WILL tut at you (they can't help it, it's some kind of built-in octogenarian reflex). It's hard not to lose your shit when every other child in the building seems to be happily munching on the free fruit they're giving out, but yours has collapsed in a sobbing heap at the patisserie counter because you won't let her have the giant chocolate lollipop covered in sprinkles…

Following on from the above, a steady stream of snacks will be required to keep the tears at bay. So yes, you will essentially be wandering around the shops to replenish the food that your child is eating… at the shops. But can you really call yourself a parent if you don't catch yourself doing something *completely* pointless at least once a day?

It's also important to remember that the majority of children are thieving gits. Only last week, I had to give chase in Boots when Orla legged it towards the exit clutching a handful of eyeliner pencils and a pack of incontinence pads (neither of which I needed, just to be clear). Sometimes, though, they leave you no choice but to suck it up and buy their ill-gotten gains. Apparently, it's quite difficult to resell chocolate lollies with teeth marks in. (Who knew??)

Another thing – you know when you go to Waitrose to buy fancy cakes that you pretend to have baked yourself (might just be me), and they have those 'Community Matters' boxes that you put your tokens in at the end to give to a good cause? Some children (naming no names) LOVE putting the tokens in, but aren't so crazy about not being able to get them out again. Nothing says 'I don't give a crap about this poxy community' like a wailing little girl desperately trying to claw their contribution back out of the *Hearing Dogs for Deaf People* slot…

Key learning point here – if shopping with your partner, DO NOT split up to save time – not only will it take you far longer to find each other again than it would have ever taken to do the shop together in the first place, but when you do finally locate your other half, your screaming womb-fruit will be hurtling down the aisle towards you in a revolving trolley (*"but she LOVES it"*…*"I can see that, but this is Morrisons, not the bloody fairground!"*) **AND** he'll have completely caved and bought her that sodding giant lollipop (which you'll no doubt be seeing again in liquid form on the car journey home).

As the minutes tick by, no matter how well prepared or good at distracting them you are, there inevitably comes a time when the whining ramps up as soon as the trolley slows down, meaning you're now frantically running about the place like Supermarket Sweep contestants:

"Grab the milk – not that one, the small one, the blue one, the SMALL BLUE ONE!"

"Don't we need tomatoes for the…"

"Just LEAVE the tomatoes!"

"But…"

"GOD DAMN IT MAN, THERE ISN'T TIME!!!"

And bloody hell those supermarket gurus are crafty – they just know that you'll be nearing the end of your tether by the time you reach the checkout, so when your child reaches out for the ridiculously over-priced Peppa Pig comic that's coincidentally RIGHT THERE, at exactly their height, you're not going to put up much of a fight. *"Oh look darling, it's the summer special, complete with 700 stickers and 20 interconnecting pieces of plastic shrapnel for us to scatter liberally across the living room floor"* – how absolutely divine.

That reminds me, I really must put my order in this week…

THE ULTIMATE 'OUT AND ABOUT' is that collective exercise in optimism over experience – the magical family holiday. You'll remember that I touched on this briefly earlier on (AKA, the great vacation vom-a-thon of 2016). Luckily, we've managed to avoid anything quite as revolting on subsequent trips, but I'd be lying if I said that we'd managed to nail anything remotely like the chilled-out family getaway of my fond (and foolish) imaginings.

We've not been brave enough to unleash Orla overseas yet, so for us, it's all about the UK staycation. Here are my top tips for anyone embarking on a lovely relaxing break with their own children this summer:

1. Immediately adjust your expectations regarding the 'relaxing' part. You will STILL be getting up at 5am, saying, "for the last time, PLEASE just PUT your BLOODY shoes on!" and trying not to explode every time they dry-heave at the sight of a vegetable. You'll just be doing it with

a prettier view and fluffier towels in the bathroom.

2. When deciding how many nights to book, don't forget to account for the fact that it will take you AT LEAST a fortnight to unpack the 20 bags of bedtime / bath time / mealtime / backup / one-more-bag-for-luck clothing you deemed 'essential' to ensure that your little one could survive 7 days in the wilds of Totnes. I seriously considered putting an offer in on our holiday cottage at the end of the week, because we'd basically moved in by that point.

3. Spraying a child head-to-toe with sun cream and letting them loose on a beach will inevitably, and apparently permanently, transform them into some kind of sand-coated toddler-goujon. Resign yourself to everything and everyone you love being covered in it for the duration of your holiday.

4. If you're going to spend hundreds of pounds on a trip to the zoo (which is seemingly unavoidable: I presume the majority of the animals are gold-plated and fart rainbows), make sure to check the weather forecast first. Otherwise, you're just *that* family who spent a fortune to stand in the pouring rain peering into deserted animal enclosures, and whose daughter, when asked about her favourite animal, opts for the absolute tank of a seagull who swooped in and stole some poor fecker's Rocky Road...

5. 10% of your time at the swimming pool will be spent in the actual pool. The other 90% will be

taken up with blowing up armbands, wrestling wriggly threenagers in and out of swimsuits every five minutes for toilet trips, breaking up pool-side fights over whose go it is to play with the inflatable turtle, and shouting "*NO RUNNING!* **DO.NOT.RUN!**" until you are hoarse.

6. Do not set ONE FOOT into a seaside arcade with an under 5 unless you're fully prepared to spend at least three hours frantically feeding £20's worth of 2p coins into a machine in pursuit of a Paw Patrol keyring.

7. If you happen to visit one of those children's adventure parks and finally gather enough courage to accompany your incredibly excited child on one of those mahoosive wavy slide things, with just a smelly old sack standing between you and certain death, it is generally frowned upon to scream "*SHIIIITTTTTTT-SHIT-SHIT-SHIT-SHIT-SHIT-SHITTTT!!*" as you make your graceful descent.

8. If, one rainy evening, when the kids are tucked up in bed and you're a few glasses of wine down, you decide to break into the token stash of well-used board games for a 'bit of fun', just remember that nobody likes a sore loser. So, if 'tipsy you' is the kind of person who throws Play-Doh at their husband during a particularly tense round of Cranium whilst aggressively shouting "*IT'S A POOL TABLE!!!! HOW CAN YOU NOT SEE IT'S A SODDING POOL TABLE?? GET YOUR HEAD IN THE GAME!!*" – maybe sit that one out.

Luckily amidst all the chaos, there will be at least one moment when the sun comes out, nobody is crying, and you can snap that essential #Blessed #FunInTheSun #Family social media photo…

TWELVE

High days and holidays

***Birthdays 101** – trying to look pleased when you unwrap a gift someone's bought your child, and it's one of those toys that you know is going to ruin your life, i.e. Shouty McFlashy Lights; the 1000 piece play set… it's tricky to simultaneously gush over how clever they were to find it, and rack your brains for the perfect counter-gift to buy when their little darling's big day rolls around (ideally something that farts glitter and plays 'It's a Small World' on a loop). #RevengeIsSweet*

When I think back to my own childhood, a lot of my happiest memories are woven around Christmas and birthdays, which really does up the emotional ante when it comes to organising those big days for your own children.

First birthdays are a bit of a doddle. They're really just an excuse for a load of adults to get together over a platter of mini quiches and congratulate you on still being able to remember your own name after surviving 365 days of parenting pandemonium on a thimble-full of sleep and a truckload of Wispa Golds.

It does get a tad trickier as they get older, though.

With Orla's 4th birthday fast approaching, she was

desperate for her very own 'Happy-Birthday-To-You with PRESENTS!!' (or 'party', as it's known to the rest of us).

There's barely enough room to swing a cat in our living room, and in any case I'm reasonably fond of my furniture pre-party-apocalypse, so the time had come to book a 'proper' kids' party.

Not going to lie, it was a bit of an experience!

My number one piece of advice – start at least 8 weeks earlier than I did, as it turns out that 99% of the suitable venues (you know the kind I mean: wipe-down surfaces, areas for the children to repeatedly run into each other and trip over invisible obstacles, a persistent whiff of parental misery), had already been booked up for the entire month of October by parents far more organised than me!

And what is with the crack-of-dawn party slots at these places? I'm sorry, but I can barely cope with my own child at 9am, I'm certainly not letting her join forces with an entire mob of pint-sized mischief-makers at stupid o'clock in the morning.

It's also vital to ignore your husband when he suggests inviting 'some of her friends from nursery'. Firstly, at her age, they're not really 'friends' so much as people she happens to be playing next to / rivals in the race to get to the slide first / snot buddies. Secondly, I've been warned by many a veteran of the birthday scene that once you jump on board the party train, it's almost impossible to get off – all the children you invited will each have their own party that you in turn must dutifully attend, leading to an endless cycle of awkward Saturday afternoons sipping warm squash and making small talk with strangers whilst inwardly praying that your rampaging little moppet (currently sky-high on life, sugar and the cries of that poor doomed little fecker who tried to touch her favourite cuddly toy) doesn't vomit all over the bouncy castle.

Decorations – do not Google 'children's party decoration ideas' unless fully prepared to be bombarded by Instagram-worthy zoo tableaus constructed entirely from balloon animals and ornately hand-embroidered bunting strung together with unicorn hairs (may have slightly exaggerated that last part). WHO HAS THE TIME??!!

Similarly, do not under any circumstances ask your child what kind of cake they would like, imagining that this will be limited to 'chocolate' or "*whichever best suits your budget / skills / timescale, mummy!*" They will almost definitely pick that three-tiered Paw Patrol monstrosity complete with fondant canine heroes and 'surprise' sweetie filling that they saw on YouTube once. She seems to have mistaken me for Mary Berry, or a gazillionaire. Either way, you're having a giraffe, love!

Whatever happened to the simple pleasures of partying on down with Ronald McDonald and those shifty-looking hamburgers on legs in your nearest fast-food basement, or lobbing a few sausage rolls and a Colin the Caterpillar cake in your guests' general direction and hoping for the best? Those were the days…

Still, it all worked out for the best. I lost my voice from repeatedly shouting "SAY THANK YOU!!", consumed my own body weight in nuggets and scotch eggs, and fully replenished our stock of oversized helium balloons (destined to float ominously around the house scaring the crap out of people for the next 6 months or so). I'd call that a roaring success!

OF COURSE, this all pales in comparison to the relentless slog-a-thon that is preparing for Christmas. This starts around September time, from which point my daughter spends every waking hour pointing to adverts /

supermarket shelves / random dogs on the street and shouting "***NEED*** *THAT FOR CHRISTMAS!*" – I'm strongly considering ditching the whole 'letter to Santa' idea and just mailing him the Argos catalogue with a *hope your elves are in shit-hot form this year, big fella!* post-it note attached.

December itself is officially the craziest month in the parenting calendar. And as if it wasn't stressful enough cobbling together your basic stocking / tree / 80-different-batteries-just-in-case Xmas paraphernalia, we're now bombarded with social media posts of elaborate North Pole breakfasts and Christmas Eve boxes and Bloody Elves on Sodding Shelves.

I don't bother with any of that stuff, but I have a particular beef with the elves.

Laziness is a major factor; after 30 rounds of pre-bedtime "*I need a wee! I'm thirsty! Is it Christmas yet? Sing Jingle Bells! But my hair isn't tired!*" sleep-avoidance antics, I'm heading straight for the sofa and the biscuit tin, not setting up intricate tableaus starring Shifty McCreepy Face pratting about with marshmallows.

But mainly, it's because it really wouldn't be fair to Orla, given that if Santa's Little Snitch was reporting back to his superior on **MY** behaviour every night, I definitely wouldn't be getting any presents! I can just hear his whiney little voice now:

Day 1 – Bit of a shock to the system here, St Nick... do you remember The Jones from Xmas 2017? Lovely family – they made that scale model of Westminster Abbey out of gingerbread and ad-libbed festive Haikus around the fireplace. Such fun. Anyway, this lot are NOTHING like that... although frankly, it's hard to make much out amidst the sea of plastic tat, Kinetic Sand and Peppa Pig merchandise rapidly swallowing up their living room.

Day 2 – The LIES Santa, the TERRIBLE, constant LIES! Just today, she told her child that if the lights are flashing on those £2-a-go ride-ons outside the supermarket, it means they're not working, AND that she has no idea where Twinkle the magical walking / talking / singing unicorn is – he's been in the bread bin for FOUR DAYS and counting, the poor little fecker...

Day 3 – Just checking in again, F.C. – too much to go into at this time of night, but safe to say she earned strike three sometime between eating the last Kinder Egg at 7am (then denying all knowledge) and calling that guy who cut her up on the A508 'an absolute spunk trumpet'.

So, best of luck with it to the rest of you, but I'm planning on staying firmly under the jolly old fella's radar until the 25th. #ElfFreeZone

THAT'S NOT to say that I won't still be absolutely slammed with Xmas admin. Here are my plans for the festive lead-up to help you keep on top of those key milestones:

DEC 1st
Vainly attempt to stop offspring consuming entire advent calendar in one go.

DEC 2nd
Reinforce strict 'No Elves on Shelves' policy. Nobody has time for that shit.

DEC 3rd
Buy Xmas biscuits and selection boxes. Congratulate self for being so organised.

DEC 4th
Accidently stress-eat Xmas biscuits and selection boxes.

DEC 5th

Secretly replenish Xmas biscuits and selection boxes.

DEC 6th

Consider cutting own ears off after 5,000[th] airing of 'All I Want For Christmas' on the radio this week.

DEC 7th

Spend magical afternoon decorating Xmas tree with family.

DEC 8th

Spend magical afternoon rearranging Xmas tree whilst family isn't looking.

DEC 9th

Join Facebook black market of mums frantically trying to swap / buy / pilfer extra nativity tickets BY ANY MEANS NECESSARY!

DEC 10th

Write out 40 nursery Christmas cards: AKA – the pointless exchange of paper between kids who cannot read, write or even pick each other out of a line-up most days.

DEC 11th

Christmas crafting session for the little ones. Spend rest of month covered in glitter, glue and cotton wool, like some kind of festive disco sheep.

DEC 12th

Write letter to Santa together. Suggest replacing 'real flying reindeer' and 'rollercoaster for the garden' with more realistic choices.

DEC 13th

Attend work Xmas party. Won't stay long, busy day tomorrow…

DEC 14th

Xmas party a bit of a blur. May have fallen into a

bush. Attempt to survive crack-of-dawn softplay party with chronic hangover.

DEC 15th

"HOW CAN IT ONLY BE 10 DAYS UNTIL XMAS!!!"

Spend afternoon panic-ordering from Amazon.

DEC 16th

Knock up some homemade mince pies. They taste like cardboard and sadness. Pop to Morrisons for edible replacements to pass off as my own.

DEC 17th

Embark on lovely wintery family walk. Quickly remember that family dislikes winter, walking, and all associated activities. Sack off lovely family walk in favour of lovely nearby pub.

DEC 18th

Sob proudly as child knee-slides her way through the nativity. Try to hide surprise when a giraffe, Chase from Paw Patrol and the three bears also wander over to the manger.

DEC 19th

Secretly replenish Xmas biscuits and selection boxes. Again.

DEC 20th

Remortgage house to visit Santa's grotto at the local garden centre. Try not to swear when child asks for a gift that has NOT ONCE been mentioned until today.

DEC 21st

Chastise self severely for forgetting to book online food delivery. Fight to the death with surprisingly strong octogenarian for the last turkey in Sainsbury's.

DEC 22nd

Become victim of own excellent hiding skills when I cannot for the life of me remember where I stashed the bloody Christmas presents...

DEC 23rd

Endless, hellish gift-wrapping cycle of misplacing the scissors, losing the end of the sellotape and questioning life choices.

DEC 24th

Stare incredulously at partner when they ask whether I've had any thoughts on what I'd like for Christmas... enjoy sweet revenge an hour later as said partner huffs and puffs his way through a 45-step toy kitchen assembly.

DEC 25th

Midnight onwards – shout, *"go back to bed, it's not Christmas yet!"* every 15 minutes before finally caving sometime around 5am.

5:30am – Fight my way through the towering tsunami of wrapping paper and plastic tat devouring the ground floor in search of the Buck's Fizz – because, you know, IT'S CHRISTMAS!!

Remainder of the day:

1 – EAT ALL THE THINGS
2 – DRINK ALL THE THINGS
3 – COLLAPSE ON SOFA

And *then* of course there's Boxing Day, devoted to near-constant grazing on leftovers and Quality Streets whilst assembling ALL the playsets and testing out ALL the craft kits and trying not to cry when it ALL goes to pot. Here's a little diary extract from last year's shenanigans:

We have been attempting to build the 'family fun' Playmobil Zoo for

approximately two hours now. We're still on step 4. Precisely NOBODY is having fun. I may have sworn several times during step 2. Mum's popped outside for a 'quick break', but I strongly suspect that she's vaulted the garden fence and made a run for it. Turns out that deciphering intricate picture instructions and jamming a thousand tiny twatting screws into a thousand tiny twatting holes in anything resembling the right order is not our strong point.
Off you fuck Playmobil, off you jolly well fuck...
#HappyBoxingDay #NoEndInSight #FamilyFun

So yes, it's a total stress-fest. Despite that (and I'm clearly a glutton for punishment in this respect), I absolutely love it. I love how her eyes light up when she's telling Father Christmas what she'd like this year. I love how excited she gets when we put up the tree. I cried with pride during her one line in the nativity (which was delivered with surprising clarity given that she said it with a face full of tea towel after messing about with her shepherd's hat one too many times), and I *love* that golden hour on Christmas Eve when everything is finally wrapped and assembled, and you can have a really satisfying 'job done' sit down before the carnage unfolds the following day.

That being said, I could definitely do without the part where she's still singing 'Away in a Manger' in March. And her absolute refusal to accept that Father Christmas has shut up shop for the year. She's come up with a cunning plan to lure him back tonight – I'm just not entirely convinced that three old carrots and a half-eaten hamburger left lovingly by the fireplace is going to be sufficiently enticing...

THIRTEEN

Where did all the time go?

I still haven't quite wrapped my head around the fact that Orla only has a few more weeks of nursery, and then she's off to school! Still got a few items on the old 'to-do' list:

- Label the bejeezus out of every item of uniform. I'm tempted to see if I can get those branded cardigans added to our contents insurance – given what the school are charging for them, they're clearly one of our most valuable possessions!

- Squeeze into Clarks with a bunch of other overheated, underprepared parents snatching for the last pair of sensible black size 10 shoes (*"no you CANNOT have Lelli-Bloody-Kelly, I do not give a monkeys that they're drenched in glitter and come with a magical make-up wand, Mummy has bills to pay and those adverts make her want to claw her own eyes out with a rusty spoon"*).

- Get over the fact that, even though she has spent less than 5 minutes in the same room as her new class teacher thus far, she already includes her in every picture she draws, talks about her incessantly, and asks whether she can come on holiday with us. Took me years to get that much of a look-in.

- Try not to get sucked into the whirlwind of panic that is the school's 'New Parents Facebook Group'… oh shit it, I've bought the wrong-coloured book bag, and EVERYBODY else has ordered lunches at least three terms in advance, and lord they're not *already* organising a whip-round are they, she hasn't even set foot on the premises yet! ANNNDDDD BREATHE…

- Work out what on earth we're going to do for childcare whilst she is 'settling in' for a grand total of 1 hour and 55 minutes a day. FOR TWO WEEKS!!! She'll be absolutely livid when I rock up less than two hours in; she's already outraged after 8+ solid hours of nursery: *"WHY ARE YOU HEREEEEEEE MUMMY!! IT'S SOOOO EARLLYYYYYY!!! COME BACK LATTTTERRRRRRR!"* #FeelingTheLove

- The above, for half terms, Christmas, summer holidays… 😬

- Come up with something slightly more creative for dinners than 'things on toast' and 'snack drawer buffet' now that she's making the rather brutal transition from luxe nursery luncheons like Thai green curry and mixed-bean enchiladas to becoming a member of the cheese-sandwich-and-a-yoghurt packed-lunch brigade.

- Find a gift for her nursery staff that adequately expresses how grateful I am to them for keeping her alive, teaching her to nap on something that's not me, doing 90% of the potty training, letting her cover somewhere that's not my house in paint and mud, giving her a safe and loving space to grow whilst I'm at work, playing a huge part in the amazing person that she has become… hmmmm, thinking about it, I'm not sure a card and a box of Celebrations is going to cut it!

I just don't know where the time has gone. Warning: another one of those annoyingly true parenting cliches coming up: the days are *long*, but the years really are short.

When you have children, Father Time is basically the enemy.

He's the guy you're mentally shaking your fist at when you once again begin your day at a time that starts with a 4, robotically inhaling caffeine whilst your fresh-as-a-daisy mini-me bounces off the furniture like a Duracell Bunny at Mardi Gras.

He's rigged it so that the longer it takes you to prepare that child-friendly risotto jam-packed with vegetables and good intentions (your ears ringing with Jamie Oliver's assurances that his kids can't get enough of the bloody stuff), the quicker you'll be scraping their untouched plate clean and wondering whether a Dairylea 'Ham N Cheese' snack pack counts as a balanced dinner.

He looms menacingly over you in the morning as you scour the living room for lost toys / your car keys / your sanity whilst simultaneously chasing your semi-naked sprog around the coffee table, mentally checking off the 101 essential items for the nursery bag, and half-heartedly lobbing wholemeal toast in their general direction in the hope that they'll accidentally take on some nutrients mid-scream.

He contrives to make that hour before bedtime, that unrelenting procession of increasingly high-pitched wails (yours) of "*I won't tell you again!*", "*Why are you licking that?!!*" and "***Right, I'm counting to 5!***" (But will stop at 4, because everyone in the room knows that there's feck all left in your parenting arsenal if you actually get there), last about a decade.

He makes five minutes' peace whizz by in a flash, whilst "*just five more minutes mummy!*" drags on for days.

But ultimately, the REALLY annoying thing about time when you're a parent, is that you know there will never be enough of it.

All of a sudden, they'll just beam at you, or hurl themselves into your arms, or do something AMAZING for the very first time, and you flip from wishing time away, to desperately trying to grasp hold of it. Because there will never be enough lazy summer days in the local park, or sticky kisses on sandy beaches. There will never be enough Christmas mornings, or snuggly Sunday breakfasts in bed, or impromptu living-room discos. I dread the time when she no longer wants to hold my hand, or runs towards me when I enter the room, or comes straight to me for cuddles when she's sad. Inevitably, all of those exhilarating 'firsts' will become bittersweet 'lasts'. And often, I haven't even realised it until that time has passed.

Time is the enemy, but also such a gift.

I do, however, spend an inordinate amount of that time feeling guilty about how much of it is 'quality time'. Weekdays are often a blurry race to the finish line filled with pick-ups and drop-offs and deadlines and "crap, is that TOMORROW?", whilst we gallop desperately towards the bath-book-bed routine. Weekends are better but seem to get swallowed up by 'the big shop' and household jobs and all manner of mundane tasks. Of course, there have been trips to the farm, meals out, that weekend at Peppa Pig World (be warned, that place is batshit crazy ALL DAY; the second those gates open parents are leapfrogging prams and hurling their offspring at the nearest available ride). Often, though, it's a trip to the park, a gander round the local garden centre and back to the house to top up the baked-beans-to-living-room-floor ratio.

I worry that we're not doing enough of the whizz-bang, magical family memories stuff; that because we haven't managed a day full of exciting / educational / creative / life-affirming jaunts and jolly japes, we're failing.

But then... I was driving Orla home last week after a rather uneventful day involving a pootle around the shops and a trip to the library. It was pouring with rain, but we were in high spirits given that we'd seen not one, but TWO yellow cars, and an excellent variety of doggies, including a Dalmatian (which, if you're as big a fan of Marshall from *Paw Patrol* as she is, is akin to clocking Taylor Swift sashaying down your local high street).

After a minute or so of silence, I caught a glimpse of her in my mirror. She was absolutely beaming in my direction.

"*Mummy?*"

"Yes baby?"

"*I am* **SO** *happy!*"

I'm not going to lie, I welled up a bit.

Times like that remind me how much of a kick she gets out of the unextraordinary everyday – like helping with the shopping list in Aldi (although I'll let you be the judge of just how helpful it is to quality-check a packet of Bourbons on the way round), or sitting on the kitchen counter asking me a million-and-one questions whilst I make dinner (again, usually working her way through my ingredients; there's definitely a pattern here).

So yes, I'm never going to stop aiming to carve out a bit more time for 'the grand family day out', but I'm also going to try to remember that in their world, the recipe for happiness can be as simple as a game of I Spy with someone you love (as long as it involves dogs; it should ALWAYS involve dogs).

A final thought on time for this chapter. As the years go by, my '*should we have another one? Is NOW the right time? Will it ever be?*' internal debate rages on. (FYI – I'm referring to children here rather than say, biscuits, as the answer would obviously be 'absolutely – finish the packet before anyone else notices').

But seriously, is there some kind of 'time for number two!' alarm that just kicks in one day? Everyone else seems so sure; "*Oh, we always knew we wanted more*" or "*nope, we're one and done!*" … is it weird to be so indecisive?

On the one hand, I always imagined having more than one – I'm from a big family myself and always pictured at least two kids running around the garden, splashing each other in the pool on summer holidays, opening their presents side by side on Christmas Day (*yes, I know that this is the rose-tinted version where I have conveniently edited out one screaming because the other looked at her funny, or sat in her space, or breathed too loudly… just let me dream)*. BUT – there's no hiding from the fact that I found that first year of motherhood incredibly tough; would it be easier the second time around, or would it break me? And then there's the logistics of it all – it takes two of us running around like headless chickens from dawn till dusk to negotiate the whole *'getting ready / work / nursery / chores / meals / tantrums / bath / more tantrums / bedtime / PLEASE go to bed / bedtime-take-two / thank fuck, she's finally asleep'* assault course that is our daily life. How does that even work when there's double trouble?

And it's not that Orla isn't enough, she's ace (a bit of an arse sometimes, but overall, I'm giving her a pretty high mark). But I worry that she might be lonely as an only child, or that it might be harder for her when we're older and there's nobody to share the load. But then again, it's not like buying an extra rabbit at Pets at Home so the other one has company, is it? She has a gaggle of cousins, lots of peer interaction at nursery, play groups etc, so she's certainly not lacking in that department at the moment.

But then AGAIN, again, they say that you never regret the things you do, only the things that you don't. And I don't feel ready to say that all these amazing 'firsts' we're experiencing with Orla will be the lasts, the onlys. And yet, I don't get that yearning 'my family isn't complete' feeling that so many other mums talk about. I know that life as a three would still be lovely, and in no way lesser, just different.

And THEN, even if we DID decide to crack on, I'm acutely aware that it's not as simple as that, we may not even be able to have another – Mother Nature can be a bit of a twunt that way. And that's not even going into the whole other question of 'when?', at which point you start bringing age gaps and house size and financials and maternity leave into the equation... eek!

I really hope that Domino's delivers to this fence that I seem to be firmly wedged on! Am I completely overthinking this, or are / were you as indecisive as I am on the subject?

FOURTEEN

Some epic developments

Fast-forward to the present day and quite a lot has changed since I penned the last chapter of this book!

For one, we're in our (second? third?) Coronavirus-related lockdown, which would have been unfathomable a year ago when we were all wondering how we were going to manage THREE WHOLE WEEKS of this before we could go back to normal.

And this lockdown is soooo much worse than the first one, which I can't help but look back on quite nostalgically. It was all a bit of a novelty then – we had lovely weather, gave ourselves hernias bunny-hopping across the living room with Joe Wicks, Sophie Ellis-Bextor was discoing around her kitchen island and everybody else was baking banana bread and clapping on doorsteps and fighting over the last bag of fusilli in Tesco. Good times.

Nowadays, cabin fever is at an all-time high, the weather is unrelentingly atrocious, and I am attempting to juggle a full-time job with home-schooling a 5 year old, which has been a real eye-opener. I've said it before, and

I'll say it again, teachers do not get paid anywhere near enough for this shit…

A DAY IN THE LIFE OF A LOCKDOWN MUM

– Woken up at the crack of dawn by a small person prising open your eyelids shouting, "*IT'S NOT LEARNING TODAY, IS IT???*" directly into your retinas.

– Prepare the first of at least three breakfasts for perpetually ravenous locked-down offspring.

– Simultaneously smear on foundation for fast-approaching work Teams meeting whilst hand-drawing today's penguin-labelling activity because the bloody printer is out of bloody ink again *(in no way connected to the fact that someone decided to print 30 pictures of dogs from the Internet half an hour previously)*. Newsflash – turns out you're crap at drawing penguins… and everything else, for that matter,

– Apologise to work colleagues for slightly distracting sight of a 5 year old in a tiger mask hokeycokeying across their screens as you recap the weekly numbers.

– Fetch snacks.

– Do some literacy work. This basically involves saying **"*FINGER SPACE!!!*"** 736 times and Googling things like 'Fisher Family Kinetic Letters' and 'Slide up to the brave monkey!' because you have not got a fecking clue what any of this has to do with writing the word 'dog'.

– Make more snacks.

– Go a few rounds of "*P - I - G, PI-G, PIIIIGGGGGG*" … "*ummm, is it potato??*" before taking a quick stroll to the kitchen to silently bash your head against the fridge door over the sheer futility of it all.

– Whilst you're there, pick up some more snacks.

– Write the same customer email 32 times because your

full attention is apparently required to debate who would win in a fight between a fridge-throwing bear and Wonder Woman.

– Maths o'clock. Try not to lose it when greeted with outright refusal to do any sums involving the number 3 because 'it's too wiggly'…

– Tell your boss you'll have to call her back in a tick whilst you locate that particular file, hoping she can't hear the dulcet tones of your little darling screaming "*WIPE MY BUM MUMMY, IT'S A MASSIVE ONE*" in the background.

– Make lunch for what seems like the 930th time this month (inevitably something out of a packet with a hearty side of 'sugar-coated crap they've been angling for since 6am but you've lost the will to argue now that it's perfectly balanced with that slice of cucumber you both know is only on the plate for decorative purposes').

– Attempt to construct a zoo with 5 toilet rolls, 3 lolly sticks and some Peppa Pig stickers. Stick the whole shebang together with two rolls of Sellotape and your own tears. Gobble down your child's paltry lunch leftovers to sustain you through your next Zoom meeting.

– Unknowingly do an entire presentation to the Sales and Marketing team with Candy Cat and Zoe Zebra stuck to your boob.

– More snacks. You're just a reception kid's snack bitch now.

– Laugh hysterically as an email pops up from school with some 'fun extra activities' you can do to celebrate national bird-watching week. Do they not know that you're still far too busy twatting about with tricky words and dreaming about decapitating Biff, Chip AND Kipper?

– Passive-aggressively text husband (currently in third consecutive Very Important Meeting upstairs) informing him that if he doesn't tag team in within the next 10 minutes you will lock them both in the office for the remainder of the afternoon with just his wits and a Paw Patrol kazoo to survive.

– Quick break for a jolly family walk in horizontal rain to the same park that you've visited every day since the beginning of time. What you wouldn't give for an hour in one of those sweaty softplay warehouses right about now…

– Check back in for today's live phonics lesson, which is absolute carnage as twenty 5 year olds run around their houses looking for something that begins with 'ch'. Mummy manages to stub her toe on the coffee table when haring off to find the 'sound of the day' cards and hopes to God she didn't just introduce an entire reception class to the phrase 'FUUUCKKK A DUCCKKKK!!!!'

– Decide to jack it all in and let your trusted co-parent 'Ryan from YouTube' take over. He's totally got this.

– Time to log off for the day. The house looks like it's been burgled, there's felt tip on the carpet, Pritt Stick in everybody's hair, and not a crumb of food left in the entire building.

Is it too early to declare half term?

HOME-SCHOOLING HORROR SHOW ASIDE, we're just enormously grateful at this point to still have jobs and our health, in awe of the NHS workers, school staff, supermarket workers and thousands of other people who have managed to keep us all afloat during this absolute shitstorm of a year, and crossing our fingers things will look a lot brighter by the summer.

Another small update for you – we've decided to make it a solid decade-plus without any shut-eye! In the end, it came down to a gut feeling that we weren't quite done yet. My timing as always is impeccable: a global pandemic really is the optimal time to be sober and emotionally challenged...

With only a couple of months to go now (thank goodness – I've reached the 'whale-like' stage alarmingly quickly this time around, although it's probably 80% banana bread), it's safe to say that it's been a rather surreal pregnancy. I've barely seen any of my family or friends, my maternity appointments have taken place in a series of bizarre locations including a hotel / spa and the bar area of the local rugby stadium (with only my trusty face mask for company), it's been months since I set foot in the office, and I did my hypnobirthing classes via Zoom. (I've heard a lot of great things about hypnobirthing so am *really* hoping that it will help me get through this birth with slightly less panicking / vomiting / mooing than last time.)

I'm excited, but also slightly bricking it, because I'm much more clued up on the realities of what awaits us in those first few months than I was with Orla. I think it's important to acknowledge, though, that it is very much OK to have a mixture of emotions about it, even though you know you'll end up with a pretty fantastic little human who EVENTUALLY stops crapping on you and pulling 24-hour sleep strikes.

Reading this back has also been pretty helpful in a way (or it would have been if I'd included any actual practical advice, damn it), because I feel like I've forgotten absolutely everything about babies. Do I have time for a crash course on how to hold them / wind them / how much milk they should be drinking / how much sleep they should be getting / the most effective post-birth remedies for your aching lady parts? Thank fuck for Google...

What I will ALWAYS try to keep in mind, though, is

this bit right here. With a bit of luck, love and trial-and-error, we have managed to raise a happy, healthy 5 year old. Colic is a distant memory, and she learnt to crawl and walk and talk in her own good time, despite my worries about whether she was getting enough tummy time or how many words she was saying compared to the rest of the Mums & Tots group. We eventually cracked potty training, ditched the dummy, and reached that unimaginable milestone of putting her to bed AWAKE, leaving the room, and not having to go back in until the all-powerful Groclock declared it was morning time. We *will* get there.

Since we announced our impending arrival, Orla has swung back and forth between wild excitement and complete indifference (9 months is an awfully long time to maintain interest in anything for a child who can't even handle the 5-second delay between videos on YouTube). She has magnanimously agreed to "play with it EVEN if it's a boy," but is insisting either way that we name them Snow Puff…

It's going to be a completely new dynamic, and a totally new set of challenges, when Snow Puff Butel finally rocks up – but I guess that's a whole different book!

About the author

I'm the mum of two gorgeous children and live with my husband and approximately 765 Pokémon cuddly toys (RIP Paw Patrol phase) in Northamptonshire.

If you're reading this, you're now one of my favourite people. As such, please come and join me on my Facebook page for more tales of the chronically sleep deprived (and hopefully lots more laughs).

If you love this book, don't keep it to yourself – please leave a review to help other mums and dads find my tiny corner of printed parenting nonsense! Your support means a huge amount to me, so thank you x

facebook.com/mummalarkey

Acknowledgements

It's been quite a journey from that first tentative post about parenting on my Facebook page to publishing AN ACTUAL BOOK! A task I rather unwisely undertook whilst juggling full-time work, my second pregnancy, and home-schooling a very stubborn 5 year old during lockdown. Without the people below, I'm not sure it would even exist.

Firstly, my husband, who has gamely agreed to my sharing the good, the bad and the ugly about our parenting experience with 5,000 strangers via my blog and supported me every step of the way. He's even read most of it, which as anyone who knows him will agree is a big deal, as generally if it's not an audio book, it ain't happening. Good idea for the future, though…

Thank you to Katie, who read some of my very first ideas and encouraged me to turn them into a blog. And my lovely friends Sophie, Vicky and Emma, who have taken the time to read various drafts of the finished article and given much valued feedback and encouragement.

To my mum, who has avidly read everything I've ever written, been unfailingly honest (and correct) about the bits that need work, and whose comments on my blog posts invariably end up being funnier than anything I've said; this may not be *War and Peace*, but I hope you're proud none the less. Thank you for believing in me.

Huge thanks to Claire Wingfield for painstakingly editing my drafts and doing all the technical wizardry required to turn a messy Word document into an actual professional thing people can buy. You're amazing.

I simply wouldn't have carried on blogging this long were it not for the fantastic community of people who have shared, supported and commented on my posts. Whenever I thought about jacking it all in to have a nap and watch *Judge Judy*, your lovely words and hilarious stories kept me going. This includes all the brilliant bloggers who have helped and supported me over the years, with a special mention for Kimberly Allan, Bethany Dempsey, Fran at Whinge Whinge Wine and Alison McGarragh-Murphy (plus The Motherload Facebook community she kindly welcomed me into as a contributor).

And of course, to my children. Do I moan about you a teensy bit over the hundred-odd pages? Sure. Do I love you more than life itself and count myself rather bloody lucky to know you? Absolutely. You're pretty much everything. Love you both x